Grades 3-4

Reader's Theater...

and So Much More!

Grades 3-4

Reader's Theater...
and So Much More!

Brenda McGee and Debbie Keiser
Cover Art and Illustrations by Brandon Bolt

Routledge
Taylor & Francis Group

NEW YORK AND LONDON

First published in 2011 by Prufrock Press Inc.

Published in 2021 by Routledge
605 Third Avenue, New York, NY 10017
2 Park Square, Milton Park, Abingdon, Oxon OX14 4RN

Routledge is an imprint of the Taylor & Francis Group, an informa business

Copyright © 2011 by Taylor & Francis Group

Production Design by Raquel Trevino

ISBN: 9781032141824(hbk)
ISBN: 9781593635008(pbk)

DOI: 10.4324/9781003237549

TABLE OF CONTENTS

TO THE TEACHER

Overview

Reader's Theater is a thinking, reading, writing, speaking, and listening experience. Readers should rely on their vocal abilities to portray a character. Students should strive for voice flexibility, crisp articulation, proper pronunciation, and projection.

These plays and skits are not meant to be staged performances. There is no need for sets, elaborate props, or costumes. However, it might be fun to add more drama to the Reader's Theaters with minimal stage direction and easy-to-find props.

If you decide you would like to make one or more of the Reader's Theaters into major productions, it is suggested that students work in committees and divide up the responsibilities of creating a live performance. This could involve everything from designing scenery to writing invitations and programs. The experience could also provide an economics lesson in using budgets and selling concessions.

These Reader's Theaters were written for all students to enjoy as they develop their senses of humor; improve their oral communication skills; increase their knowledge of content; gain fluency, comprehension, and self-confidence; and boost their interest in reading.

The Reader's Theater Language Arts Skills listed on the next page will be practiced during the performance of all of the Reader's Theaters. Students will also have opportunities to use writing, research, and other skills as they complete pre, post, and extension activities found in each play.

Management

Scan the plays and assign parts you believe would fit a student's comfort level based on his or her reading ability.

Give students an opportunity to read their parts silently and ask questions about any unfamiliar words. The objective is fluency and oral expression, not cold reading.

1

If there are too many characters, assign students with smaller parts more than one character. If you have too few parts, cut some of the longer parts into more than one part. Another option is to challenge students, as a class or in small groups, to create more characters and add more parts.

Even the most reluctant and shy students enjoy Reader's Theaters. This is "learning can be fun" at its best!

Reader's Theater Language Arts Skills

Sight-Word Reading
✦ Reads numerous high-frequency words fluently

Vocabulary Development
✦ Learns new vocabulary by listening, reading, or receiving instruction

Comprehending What Is Read
✦ Uses context clues to determine words' meanings
✦ Predicts and verifies outcomes
✦ Recognizes and analyzes characters, setting, and plot in a passage listened to or read
✦ Makes and explains inferences and supports them with evidence from text
✦ Identifies facts and details
✦ Identifies the main idea (explicit and implicit) of a passage
✦ Draws conclusions and supports them with evidence from the text

Literary Response
✦ Retells a story without using the book, including beginning, middle, and end
✦ When retelling a story, includes important events and details
✦ Summarizes or paraphrases text
✦ Identifies the correct sequence of events in a story through retelling or acting out

Oral Communication
✦ Speaks to an audience using appropriate volume and rate
✦ Adapts oral language to purpose, audience, and occasion
✦ Presents dramatic interpretations
✦ Presents to an audience

Listening Skills

◆ Listens actively and purposefully

◆ Listens to, enjoys, and appreciates spoken language

Humor Terms in Literature

Exaggeration—to make something greater than it actually is; to stretch or magnify the truth

Farce—an exaggerated comedy based on broadly humorous situations; a play intended only to be funny; an absurd or ridiculous situation

Figure of speech—any phrase or saying that is not meant to be taken literally, including idioms, hyperbole, and the like

Hyperbole—an exaggeration in writing used to make a point

Idiom—a phrase that has a particular meaning other than its literal (word-for-word) meaning

Irony—when the audience expects a certain thing to happen, but then the opposite happens

Metaphor—a literary device in which two unlike things are compared without using "like" or "as"

Onomatopoeia—words that sound like the noises they describe, such as "swish," "woof," and "splat"

Oxymoron—a literary device in which two contradictory words are used together to describe something

Parody—a literary or artistic work that imitates the characteristic style of an author; a work for comic effect or ridicule

Pun—the humorous use of a word or words that are formed similarly or sound alike, but that have different meanings, made in order to play on two or more of the possible applications; a play on words

Sarcasm—a taunting, sneering, cutting, or caustic remark; a gibe or jeer, generally ironic

Satire—a manner of writing that mixes a critical attitude with wit and humor in an effort to improve humankind and human institutions

Simile—a literary device in which a comparison is made between two things using either "like" or "as"

Understatement—expressing an idea with less emphasis or in a lesser degree than is called for; the opposite of hyperbole; mostly used for ironic emphasis

Notes

_____

_____

_____

_____

_____

_____

_____

_____

_____

_____

_____

_____

Act 1

READER'S THEATERS

VOLUNTEER?

Pre-Reading Suggestions:

Assessing Prior Knowledge
◆ Ask students what a volunteer is.
◆ Have students brainstorm places they could volunteer or places that depend on volunteers.

Making Predictions
◆ "Volunteer?" is the title of this Reader's Theater. Why do students think it has a question mark at the end? What could this skit be about?

Post-Reading Suggestions:

Research
◆ Have students find out what requirements (e.g., age, grade, adult supervision, parental consent) are necessary to do the kind of volunteer work they would most like to do.

Expressing Ideas in Writing
◆ Have students write a paragraph describing their most embarrassing moment. Assure students they will not have to share unless they wish.
◆ Have students add more speaking parts to the Reader's Theater.
◆ Have students write a Reader's Theater about an experience a volunteer has during a day that isn't going very well.

VOLUNTEER?

Note to Teacher

✦ Divide students into groups of three. Have students decide which parts they will play. Have students read the skit silently, and then in groups.

✦ At the conclusion of the Reader's Theater, challenge students to analyze the humor. Why was it funny?

Cast of Characters
Coordinator
Volunteer 1
Volunteer 2

Setting
Office

Optional Props
Nametag for Coordinator

Coordinator: Hi, I'm the Volunteer Coordinator at the zoo. What brings you to see me?

Volunteer 1: Well, my friend and I would like to become volunteers for the zoo.

Coordinator: That's great! We have lots of exciting things going on here.

Volunteer 2: We love excitement, just as long as we don't have to talk to people or do anything messy.

Coordinator: Well, I'm sorry. Your job and mine both deal with giving people tours, which means you'll have to talk to people, and when you work with animals, there are always "messy" things to do.

Volunteer 1: Well, I really need the job. What does it pay?

Coordinator: The job pays nothing. That's why it's called volunteer work.

Volunteer 2: Do I have to know a lot about animals?

Coordinator: Not necessarily, but you have to be willing to learn.

Volunteer 1: I just don't know. Now, tell me again about the pay . . .

Coordinator: Look, the job doesn't pay. You help me set up special projects, tell people about the animals, prepare food for some of the animals, and explain how zoos work. Are you interested?

Volunteers: Guess not. Maybe we'll try our luck at the art museum. I understand they have a Volunteer Coordinator there, too.

Coordinator: (*rolls eyes and groans*)

WAITING ROOM

Pre-Reading Suggestions:

Prediction

✦ Have students discuss what a play entitled "Waiting Room" could be about. Record responses on the board.

Point of View

✦ Tell students this play is written from an unusual point of view (way of telling a story). Ask students what different points of view they could use to write a play entitled "Waiting Room."

Assessing Prior Knowledge

✦ Explain that this play takes place in a veterinarian's waiting room. Ask students to brainstorm the kinds of animals that might be seen in a veterinarian's office and the kinds of care that might be provided.

Post-Reading Suggestions:

Expressing Ideas in Writing

✦ Have students work in small groups to rewrite the ending to the play. Encourage them to share with their groups.
✦ Challenge students to write four additional parts, for either human or animal characters.
✦ Introduce the concept of puns. Have students identify the puns in the story, then encourage them to create more.
✦ Tell students to imagine that this play had been set in the veterinarian office of a zoo. Ask how the play might have been different.

Discriminating Between Fiction and Nonfiction

✦ After explaining the differences between fiction and nonfiction, have students discuss in what category this play falls.

Vocabulary Development

✦ Invite students to list the new words they learned from this play.

Literary Response

✦ Have teams of students retell the story in the correct sequence. Challenge students to find at least three places where puns are used.

Creating Graphic Sources to Gather and Organize Information

✦ Take a survey of the class to see what types of pets students own. Graph the results. Challenge students to create word problems for one another based on the class's graph.

WAITING ROOM

Note to Teacher

✦ There are 20 parts in this play. The Beagle has the biggest part and should be assigned to a strong reader. Assign parts, then let students practice reading, first silently, and then to a partner. Avoid asking students to read aloud without time to practice.

✦ At the conclusion of the Reader's Theater, challenge students to add more characters, rewrite some of the parts, or to analyze the humor (why was the play funny?).

Cast of Characters

Beagle	Duck
Mastiff	Vet Receptionist
Chihuahua	Finch
Ferret	Rabbit
Iguana	Alley Cat
Persian Cat Mom	Human 2
Persian Kitten 1	Vet Technician
Persian Kitten 2	Human 3
Persian Kitten 3	Poodle
Human 1	Cow

Setting

Waiting room at a veterinarian's office

Optional Props

Signs worn by actors to identify characters

Beagle: Hey, big fella, what are you in for?

Mastiff: I've got a problem with one of my teeth. (*paws at mouth*) Hurts like anything.

Beagle: Gosh, you wouldn't think a little tooth would bring a big guy like you down.

Mastiff: Well, it does. What are you in for?

Beagle: Oh, I'm just in for my yearly checkup. When you stick your nose into as many places as I do, you can't be too careful.

Chihuahua: (*shaking nervously*) Could you two please keep the noise down?

Beagle: What's your problem?

Chihuahua: Nothing!

Beagle: Oh, come on. You must be here for a reason.

Chihuahua: Well, if you must know, I am being treated for a nervous disorder.

Mastiff: A what?

Chihuahua: I get very nervous when I'm alone—and when I am around people, and when I am around other animals.

Beagle: So if you're nervous when you're alone, and around people, and around animals, then when are you NOT nervous?

Chihuahua: That's just it. I'm nervous all the time. Now just leave me alone. Pretend I'm not here. (*covers eyes with paws*)

Ferret: (*holding one paw*) I don't know what all of you have to complain about. I'm the one with a real problem. I got my paw stuck in a mousetrap that was waaaayyy up under the refrigerator. It wasn't easy to get to, I can tell you that!

Mastiff: Then why did you try?

Ferret: Because it's my nature. I'm VERY curious.

Beagle: (*looks disgusted*) Oh, brother!

Ferret: (*looking up*) Hey, what kind of animal are you?

Iguana: (*speaking slowly and occasionally sticking tongue out*) I am an iguana. I think that is pretty obvious.

Chihuahua: (*shaking*) Ask him to stop sticking out his tongue. He is making me nervous.

Beagle: What are you in for?

Iguana: That should also be obvious. I'm having a skin problem. I'm usually quite handsome.

Persian Cat Mom: I'll have to take your word on that.

Iguana: Beauty is in the eye of the beholder, madam.

Persian Kitten 1: (*in whiny voice*) Where are we, mom?

Persian Kitten 2: (*in tiny voice*) Why are we here, mom?

Persian Kitten 3: (*in small, upset voice, and spitting*) Get your tail out of my mouth!

Persian Cat Mom: Behave, you three! You are here for the first of your (*spelling out*) S-H-O-T-S that will prevent you from getting some terrible diseases.

Persian Kitten 1: What does S-H-O-T-S mean?

Persian Kitten 2: Will it hurt, mom?

Persian Kitten 3: Hey, that's MY ear you are chewing on!

Human 1: (*frantic*) Excuse me! Coming through! I have an emergency!

Ferret: What's he got wrapped up in that jacket? I've got to find out.

Beagle: (*sniffing the air*) Smells foul to me!

Human 1: This duck swallowed a fishhook. You can see the fishing line coming out of its mouth.

Duck: (*quacking and making choking sounds*) I just wanted a nice piece of bread, no strings attached—but NO! (*choking again*) I get a fishhook with this piece!

Human I: I'm really sorry. I was using bread for bait. I didn't think about ducks liking bread, too.

Vet Receptionist: We'll take care of him. Will you just have a seat in the waiting room? I'll see what the veterinarian suggests we do.

Finch: (*making chirping sounds*) Humans sure can be thoughtless sometimes. I know. This one time, I was flying around the den and thought I saw some fresh fruit on the coffee table. You'll never believe what was inside the fruit!

Iguana: I'll bite. What was it made of?

Finch: Wax. Cold, solid, tasteless wax. I had stomach problems for a week! See what I mean about humans being thoughtless?

Rabbit: I don't think all humans are thoughtless. My human takes great care of me!

Ferret: Then why are you here?

Rabbit: To get my nails clipped.

Mastiff: You come to the doctor to have your nails clipped? (*shakes head in disbelief*)

Rabbit: Well, my human is very cautious. If you clip my nails too short, it can cause a lot of pain and bleeding. My human doesn't want that to happen, so I come in every couple of months to have the professionals do it.

Chihuahua: Stop talking about clipping nails. That makes me nervous, too!

Persian Kitten I: Is it our turn next?

Persian Kitten 2: Are you sure it won't hurt?

Persian Kitten 3: Get off my face!

Persian Cat Mom: Shh! It won't be much longer.

Iguana: Check out the new guy.

Alley Cat: (*angry and tough*) You talkin' to me?! You talkin' to me?! Hey, you talkin' to me?!

Iguana: Yes, obviously. You just came in. I am talking to you.

Alley Cat: (*to Persian Cat Mom*) Hey, mama, how ya doin'?

Ferret: So, new guy, what are you here for?

Alley Cat: None of your business. How's that for an answer?

Human 2: I'm here to drop off my male cat to be neutered. When should I come back to pick him up?

Persian Kitten 1: Mom, what does "neuter" mean?

Persian Kitten 2: Does that hurt?

Persian Kitten 3: Get me out of this basket!

Vet Receptionist: He'll be ready first thing in the morning. Have a nice day!

Alley Cat: Yeah! (*shaking head*) Nice day for you, maybe.

Human 1: Have you heard anything about the duck yet?

Vet Technician: Yes, the vet says it was great that you brought the duck in. She said many people would feel guilty and run away, or wouldn't care and would just leave the duck. She wants to know if you would be willing to take the duck back to its home as soon as she is finished. It won't be much longer, and there will be no charge.

Human 1: Sure, that's the least I can do.

Rabbit: See what I mean? There are lots of nice humans around.

Human 3: I'm here to pick up my sweet little poodle, Foxy Lady. I left her here while I went to Paris, and I'm ready to take her home now.

Vet Technician: I'll bring her right out.

Poodle: (*sounding very spoiled*) Don't ever leave me here again! There's nothing but animals here! I didn't like the food, and the accommodations were practically nonexistent! No cushions! No television! No snacks! I had to WALK on the cement in the sun! (*whines and whimpers*)

Finch: Check out the pink bows on her ears!

Poodle: Do you see what I mean? This is the kind of harassment I've had to put up with all week! If I don't get home soon, I think I will just faint from all the stress!

Duck: OK, where's the big, brave fisherman? You owe me a ride back home, buddy—and a MAJOR apology!

Chihuahua: It is getting too crowded in this waiting area. I'm really getting nervous now.

Rabbit: You think it's crowded now? Look what's coming through the door, everybody!

Cow: *Moooove* out of my way! I'm about to have a cow!

(*everyone scatters*)

UNUSUAL DINNER GUESTS

Pre-Reading Suggestions:

Assessing Prior Knowledge

✦ Have students define "unusual." What synonyms could be used instead of unusual?

✦ Ask students what the word "unusual" could mean in relation to the title of the play.

Making Predictions

✦ The title of this skit is "Unusual Dinner Guests." Ask students to predict what this skit is about.

Post-Reading Suggestions:

Fluency

✦ Challenge students to list as many famous people as they can in 10 minutes. Have students work with partners or in small groups, and adjust the time limit as is appropriate for age level. Next, have students place each person listed in categories (e.g., athletes, scientists, entertainers, authors).

Expressing Ideas in Writing

✦ Have students create a different ending for the Reader's Theater.

✦ Have students add to the play.

Research

✦ Have students rewrite the play by selecting three different famous people. An Independent Research sheet has been provided as a guide.

Timelines

✦ Challenge students to create a timeline that includes all of the people in this play.

UNUSUAL DINNER GUESTS

Note to Teacher

✦ If you delete the last line of this play, you have an ending. If you keep the last line of the play, you can have students continue to create an impromptu ending or write to develop a different ending.

Cast of Characters
Student 1
Student 2
Elvis Presley
Abraham Lincoln
J. K. Rowling

Setting
Dining room or kitchen

Optional Props
Signs worn by actors to identify characters

Student 1: Have you ever had someone ask you whom you would invite to dinner if you could invite anyone, from either the past or the present?

Student 2: Yeah, but I couldn't think of anybody.

Student 1: Nobody? Not one person who you would love to sit down with and have a conversation?

Student 2: No. Is that so weird? OK, who would YOU pick?

Student 1: I would pick Abraham Lincoln, J. K. Rowling, and Elvis Presley.

Student 2: You're kidding. What a bizarre group. What could those people possibly have in common?

Student 1: You would be surprised. I would just love to sit down and talk to them.

Student 2: OK. Let's suppose this was actually possible. How might the conversation go?

Student 1: Well, it might go a little something like this . . .

Elvis Presley: What's for supper? I don't want you to go to any trouble. I'd be happy with a peanut butter and 'nana sandwich.

Abraham Lincoln: I'm familiar with bananas and sandwiches, sir, but I don't know what peanut butter is. I might like to try that.

J. K. Rowling: Well, I'd prefer fish and chips, but bananas and peanut butter would be magical.

Student 1: Actually, I was going to get each of you a Happy Meal™. Would that do?

Abraham Lincoln: Certainly, young man. I would enjoy being happy.

Elvis Presley: Cool! Thank you, thank you very much.

J. K. Rowling: Since we are in America, why not? That would be charming!

Student 1: Now that the meal is settled, I'd like to ask you a question that has really been on my mind. Mr. President, looking back on your life, what are you most proud of?

Abraham Lincoln: Most people would probably say the Emancipation Proclamation. And I am very proud of that accomplishment—although I wish I had given it a different name, as it is very difficult to say. But at this point, I am most proud to have had an honorable Presidency. I believe time has shown that I set the bar very high when it came to honesty, integrity, dedication, and hats. I'm sure all of this had a lot to do with my humble beginnings.

Elvis Presley: You know, Mr. President, I was involved in the Civil Rights Movement early in my career. I'm proud of that. I also showed people that with a lot of hard work and dedication and a tacky wardrobe, a poor country boy like myself could become an international sensation.

J.K. Rowling: And I suppose I also qualify as a role model. I was actually an unemployed single mom living on government aid when I had my first book published. I was told recently that I am the first writer to become a billionaire. I guess you could say we all serve as role models. I think that is enchanting!

Student 2: OK . . . I get it. I suppose seemingly unrelated people from different periods in history, and even from different parts of the country, DO have things in common.

Student 1: Right. Now, back to my original question. Who would YOU pick to have a conversation with?

UNUSUAL DINNER GUESTS INDEPENDENT RESEARCH

Directions:

Select a famous person to research. Read at least one biography and research one additional source. Use the following research form.

Famous person: _____

Why is this person famous? _____

_____

What is unique about this person? _____

_____

When did this person live? _____

_____

Script to be inserted in the Reader's Theater: _____

_____

_____

_____

Where should the script be inserted, and how will it connect to the flow of the play? _____

_____

_____

_____

_____

RAINFOREST DETOUR

Pre-Reading Suggestions:

Assessing Prior Knowledge
✦ Create a K-W-L chart to find out what the students know, what they want to know, and (to be filled in later) what they have learned. Ask students to fill in the first two columns of the chart. What do they already know about the rainforest? What would they like to know about the rainforest?
✦ Challenge students to brainstorm a list of vocabulary words that might be associated with the study of a rainforest.

Post-Reading Suggestions:

Drawing Conclusions
✦ Have students fill in the remaining column on the K-W-L chart. Ask students what they learned about the rainforest.

Expressing Ideas in Writing
✦ Challenge students to work in small groups to rewrite the ending of this play. Allow time for sharing with the class.
✦ Challenge students to create four additional parts for this play.
✦ Have students write a paragraph identifying which animal they would be if they lived in the rainforest, and why.

Vocabulary Development
✦ Have students list the new words they learned from this play.

Geography Research
✦ Have students research the amount of rain that falls during a one-year period in a rainforest.
✦ Have students draw pictures showing the amount of sunlight that shines in each layer of the rainforest.
✦ Challenge students to show where the world's rainforests are located.
✦ Have students draw and identify the four layers of a rainforest, and then list or draw some of the plants and animals that can be found in each layer.

RAINFOREST DETOUR

Cast of Characters

Parrot 1
Parrot 2
Spider Monkey 1
Cat
Spider Monkey 2
Anteater
Ant Bird
Boa
Sloth

Bat
Howler Monkey 1
Howler Monkey 2
Katydid 1
Katydid 2
Iguana 1
Iguana 2
Capybara
Puma

Setting

An airplane landing strip in the middle of a rainforest, where an airplane has just dropped off a pet carrier containing a drowsy housecat

Optional Props

Signs worn by actors to identify animal characters

Parrot 1: (*squawking*) ROK! Would you look at that? What is that?

Parrot 2: Hey, there's something inside—ROK!

Parrot 1: You should go see what it is.

Parrot 2: No way. Let's send someone else. Hey, Spider Monkey, go see what's in that box over there.

Spider Monkey 1: Sure. We were wondering what's in there, too. (*leaps to the pet carrier*)

Cat: (*lets out long, mean meow and a couple of hisses*)

Spider Monkey 2: Better get away from it, quick! Sounds like some sort of tiger or jaguar.

Cat: (*yawns and stretches*) I most certainly am not a tiger or a jaguar, though I am a member of the feline family. May I inquire who you are and what you are doing staring at me? As you can see, you have upset me.

Spider Monkey 1: We weren't staring—we were just curious. We've never seen anything like you in the rainforest.

Cat: The what forest? You mean this isn't San Francisco?

Spider Monkey 2: Nope! You're in trouble, kitty. San Francisco is about 1,500 miles that way (*points*) . . . or that way. (*points in the opposite direction*)

Cat: Oh my gosh! This is not good. I ate my last Classy Cat Tender Morsels Cheese Snack and am completely out of catnip. What shall I eat? Where shall I live? Who shall look after me? I've never been on my own before.

Spider Monkey 1: Hey, we can help. We can tell you about where we live and what we eat, and then you can decide where you want to live. But you are going to have to take care of yourself! That's what being "wild" is all about.

Cat: Although I am not "wild" about that idea, I suppose I need to do something. Where do you live?

Spider Monkey 2: We live in the trees, in the canopy and sometimes the emergent layers of the rainforest, and we eat the fruits we find there. How does that sound?

Cat: Well, I think I could get used to living in the trees, as long as I don't have to go too high. I don't know about fruit. I think I'm more of a carnivore than an herbivore. Anybody like that around here?

Anteater: Look no further! I live on the forest floor, and I eat juicy, tasty ants.

Ant Bird: If I didn't know better, I would swear you were a pig instead of an anteater. You hog all of the tasty ants on the forest floor, so I have to eat the ones that climb the trees in the understory layer.

Anteater: Too bad, sweetheart. You snooze, you lose!

Cat: It sounds like there's too much competition for your food, so I think I'll keep looking. Thanks anyway.

Boa: Sssay, how would you like to sssee where I live and sssleep? It'sss the bessst place around!

Sloth: (*speaking very slowly*) Yeah, right! Go with him, and it will be the last time we see you. Come live with me. I'll teach you to hang upside down to do EVERYTHING.

Cat: Living with the boa is definitely out, and I don't think I could ever learn to hang upside down to sleep. But thank you both for your offers.

Bat: Hey, up here. I'm a bat, and like you, I'm nocturnal. Could you guys hold it down? I'm trying to sleep. Later tonight, I'll teach you to search for nectar. Nectar is delicious!

Cat: But you hang upside down to sleep, too. Besides, I can't fly.

Howler Monkey 1: (*shouting*) Hey! I think she should come live with us! She would fit right in. Howl!

Howler Monkey 2: (*shouting*) I think we could even teach her to howl and swing in the trees. Howl!

Cat: (*hands over ears*) I hate to interrupt, but I don't think I could ever get used to the volume at which you speak. Don't you ever talk quietly?

Howler Monkeys: NO! Howl!

(*katydids chirping*)

Cat: Excuse me, but who just made that noise?

Katydid 1: Katydid.

Cat: Oh. What are you?

Katydid 2: Katydid.

Cat: No, I want to know what kind of animal you are.

Iguana 1: They just told you.

Cat: Told me what?

Katydids: (*shouting*) KATYDID!

Cat: Katie did what?

Iguana 2: They are katydids. They just say "katydid," all day, every day. You wouldn't be happy trying to talk to them or doing anything else with them. Why don't you come live with me? I live on and near the forest floor, and I eat insects.

Cat: Insects don't agree with my delicate stomach, but thanks anyway. (*to herself*) Is everyone here creepy, or what?

Capybara: I'm the largest rodent in the world, and I eat grass. How does that sound?

Cat: WOW! I have my answer! You are, beyond a doubt, the largest rodent I have ever seen.

Capybara: I'm not just any rodent. I'm a capybara.

Cat: (*disappointed and discouraged*) Well, when I eat grass, I usually do it to help myself cough up a fur ball. I think I'm running out of options.

Puma: I suppose I could let you join my family, though we don't eat cat food. We track our food, kill it, eat the parts we want, and leave the rest. We live wherever we want.

Cat: I don't think that will work for me, either. Killing my own food would be gross! I can't even watch the Nature Channel. Eating dead things—blah!

All Animals: What's that? I hear something! Sounds like a plane.

Cat: Oh, thank goodness . . . They've come back for me! I could never live here! Hurry! Please! (*climbs back into carrier*)

(*plane lands and picks up carrier*)

Howler Monkey 1: Don't forget to write!

Howler Monkey 2: (*rolls eyes at Howler Monkey 1*) Like you could read it.

PET SHOP

Pre-Reading Suggestions:

Vocabulary Development

✦ Tell students they will perform a Reader's Theater involving different breeds of dogs. Ask them to define "breed" and "species."

Assessing Prior Knowledge

✦ Tell students there are approximately 150 different breeds of dogs. Have students work with partners or in small groups to brainstorm as many dog breeds as possible.

Point of View

✦ Ask students if they have ever gone "shopping" for a new pet. Have them imagine what the animals are thinking when they see humans examining and watching them.

Post-Reading Suggestions:

Research

✦ Every dog breed is assigned to one of seven groups or classes based on the uses for which its breed was originally developed. Have students discover what these categories are.

Expressing Ideas in Writing

✦ After determining why certain breeds were developed, students can consider whether the reasons that a particular breed was developed may now be obsolete. Have students write paragraphs explaining which breeds no longer serve their original purposes.

✦ Have students write a persuasive paragraph to convince people looking for a dog to go to a rescue group or a shelter instead of to a breeder.

✦ Ask students the following question: If you were going to create a new breed of dog, what purpose would your breed serve, and what would you call it? Write a paragraph explaining your rationale, and then draw an illustration of your dog breed.

Mathematics

◆ Have students go online and identify the cost of buying a puppy that is purebred. Then have students research the costs, for purebred dogs, of veterinary needs, food, collars, bowls, leashes, identification badges, and American Kennel Club (AKC) registration. Compare and contrast the cost of a registered dog with that of an animal adopted from a shelter.

PET SHOP

Note to Teacher

✦ This short skit explores a pet shop experience from a completely different point of view.

✦ After students read the skit, have them use the Pet Shop Independent Research sheet to explore the pros and cons of how different pets live with different kinds of people in different environments.

✦ Have students add more dog breeds to this Reader's Theater or completely rewrite the script using a variety of pets that may or may not include dogs.

Cast of Characters

Customer	Doberman Pinscher
Store Owner	St. Bernard
Assistant	German Shepherd
Beagle	Golden Retriever
Pointer	Irish Setter
Labrador Retriever	Chow
Collie 1	Spaniel
Collie 2	

Setting

Pet shop

Optional Props

Signs to identify characters/dog breeds
Chairs representing cages to stand behind

Customer: Excuse me. I am looking for a dog. Can you help me?

Store Owner: Sure, I'll try to help you, but this isn't your usual pet shop. You see, in this pet shop, the dog will pick YOU out. My assistant will show you around (*points to assistant*).

Assistant: Hi. (*shakes hands*) I'm Tom. I'll show you around. Come with me.

Customer: (*looking excited*) I can't wait to see which dog picks me!

Assistant: Don't let them hear you say "dog." They prefer the proper name Canidae, from the Latin "canis," meaning "dog." Here is the first group.

Beagle: Hi! I'm Bob, a Beagle. (*sniffs Customer*)

Pointer: I'm Bob's friend Pete. I'm a Pointer. (*points all over room*)

Beagle: We both love to track things.

Pointer: We smelled you coming. (*sniffs loudly*)

Beagle: We were able to do this because we have long noses. That's how we can pick up scents so well.

Pointer: We can actually smell things better than we can see them.

Beagle: Do you like to hunt?

Customer: No.

Pointer: Well, then we're not the dogs for you.

Assistant: Let's move on.

Labrador Retriever: Hi! My name is Elvis. I'm a Labrador Retriever, and I love to swim! I'm the best swimmer you will find. I do it by moving just my front legs. You probably call it the "doggie paddle."

Customer: I don't like to swim.

Labrador Retriever: I would definitely not be happy with you. (*walks away looking disappointed*)

Assistant: Come on.

Collie I: Hi! I'm Cary Collie.

Collie 2: I'm Candy Collie. You might have heard of my well-known cousin, Lassie.

Collie 1: Our ancestors date back to 1,000 B.C.

Collie 2: We helped farmers herd sheep, goats, and cattle.

Collie 1: Even though we are mostly brown, farmers and shepherds preferred us white so that they wouldn't confuse us with wolves and kill us by mistake. Do you have anything we can herd?

Customer: Just my brother and sister.

Collie 2: (*shaking head in disappointment*) Nope, that won't do.

Assistant: (*frustrated*) Let's move on.

Doberman Pinscher: (*growls*) I'm Spike. I'm a Doberman Pinscher. I like to guard things. I'm from Germany.

St. Bernard: I'm Beth. I'm a St. Bernard. I love to rescue people who get lost in the snow.

German Shepherd: I'm Sam Shepherd. I'm also from Germany, and I help people with visual impairments get around safely. Some of my other family members help the police.

Doberman Pinscher: (*growls furiously*)

St. Bernard: Spike! Stop that!

Doberman Pinscher: Sorry, old habit. Do you need us to help you with anything?

St. Bernard: Yes, please let us help.

German Shepherd: (*looks anxious*) I live to help!

Customer: No, I don't need any help. Sorry.

Golden Retriever: (*has something in his mouth*) Pssst! Hey, kid, come here. I'm a Golden Retriever. I love to fetch things.

Irish Setter: Me too, laddie. Do ya happen to have a stick with ya?

Customer: (*searches pockets*) No. (*looks disappointed*)

Golden Retriever: That's too bad. People call us sporting dogs. We retrieve things, and we point out birds for hunters.

Irish Setter: Do you have a kennel, laddie?

Customer: No, I want my dog to live inside.

Golden Retriever: That won't do! We like it outside.

Customer: (*looks very disappointed*) This is not going very well!

Assistant: I have to admit, you are a challenge. But we still have a few left.

Chow: I'm perfect for you. I'm a Chow. My ancestors have been around for 3,000 years. You can run your fingers through my long, thick hair, and I can lick you with my blue-black tongue. I just love cold arctic breezes. You do live in a cold, arctic climate, don't you?

Customer: Well, not exactly.

Chow: Well, then I don't exactly want to own you.

Customer: This is really embarrassing.

Assistant: OK, there is one breed left, the Toy Spaniel. They are all 12 inches or shorter.

Spaniel: Hi! I'm a Toy Spaniel, a royal favorite. My ancestors owned King Charles. I'm from England originally, and I get along great with people. Do you have any royal blood?

Customer: No. Is that a problem?

Spaniel: (*rolls eyes*) What do you think? (*walks off with nose in air*)

Store Owner: So, how is it going? Any of the dogs like you?

Customer: No.

Store Owner: (*looking sympathetic*) Have you considered getting a cat?

PET SHOP

Directions:

Select an animal that could be a potential pet. Use the following research form.

Pet: _____

Why would this animal be a good pet? _____

_____

_____

What environment would be best for this type of pet? _____

_____

_____

Where is this animal originally from? _____

_____

_____

In what ways has this animal changed over time, if at all? _____

_____

_____

_____

A BUDDHA-FUL PLAY

Geography

✦ Have students map the geographic areas where Buddha, Confucius, the Dalai Lama, Moses, Jesus, Muhammad, and other religious founders traveled.

A BUDDHA-FUL PLAY

Note to Teacher

✦ This Reader's Theater personifies some of the problems, solutions, issues, and concerns of modern society. These same issues between people have existed since the beginning of recorded history. Help students to see the meaning of the play: Happiness and contentment cannot be bought or earned through outward works or through being in control. Rather, happiness and contentment come from thinking of others before oneself and from remembering that words—even harsh ones—are gifts from others, to be either accepted or ignored.

Cast of Characters

Narrator   Mr. and Mrs. Greedy
Student 1   Mr. and Mrs. Pain
Student 2   Mr. and Mrs. Perfect
Student 3   Mr. and Mrs. Order and Control
Buddha   Mr. and Mrs. Mean

Setting

A garden retreat, India, 485 B.C.

Optional Props

Signs worn by actors to identify their characters

Narrator: About 2,500 years ago, there lived a man who was called Buddha, or Enlightened One. Thousands of people listened to his teachings. He started the religion of Buddhism. His influence is still strong in his native country of India, and his beliefs have spread to our country, as well.

Students 1, 2, and 3: Great Teacher, a small party of travelers has stopped nearby. We see five people.

Buddha: Welcome them all. Ask them if they need anything.

Student 1: They want only cool water, a warm fire, and a place to sleep for the night.

Buddha: Nothing else?

Mr. Greedy: Well . . . now that you mention it, I could use plenty more! I could do with a great feast, a goblet that's never empty, and some fun.

Buddha: Is that really what you want?

Mrs. Greedy: Of course! Why else do you think we would come to this great city? Because here, we can make enough money to buy all of the things we want.

Buddha: I once lived the life of a rich prince.

Mr. Greedy: Excellent! Then we understand each other. Wealth and pleasure—the only way to go.

Buddha: But this kind of greed never ends. You will never be satisfied. The more you get, the more you will want.

Mr. and Mrs. Pain: We do not seek wealth and pleasure. We seek inner peace and happiness.

Buddha: And how do you seek it?

Mrs. Pain: Through lots of pain and suffering.

Buddha: I once lived like that. Seeds and grass were my food. I wore clothes made of old cloth, stood still for long hours, laid upon thorns, and did not bathe, so I looked like an old tree.

Mr. Pain: Did this not give you a great feeling of peace and happiness?

Buddha: No. It only brought me foolish pride and attention from others.

Mr. Perfect: The only way to find true inner peace is by performing religious rituals perfectly.

Student 3: What do you mean?

Mrs. Perfect: We are going to the holy city to perform the proper rituals in the perfect way.

Buddha: And if along the way, you pass through a desert and meet a blind man seeking water, what will you do?

Mr. Perfect: If we have enough water, we will share some with him.

Student 2: If you do not have enough, will you help him find some?

Mrs. Perfect: Of course, if we are near our destination.

Buddha: And if you are far from your destination?

Mr. Perfect: We will ask someone else to assist him. He will understand that we must hurry to the holy city.

Mr. Order and Control: What kind of religion is that? Religion should build sincerity, not selfish convenience. Sincerity is what you should be looking for.

Student 1: Tell us more.

Mrs. Order and Control: Where we come from, we have learned to improve and strengthen our communities.

Student 2: And how is this done?

Mr. Order and Control: By raising leaders who are noble and honest.

Student 3: Certainly. But where do you find such leaders? We think you are dreamers.

Mrs. Order and Control: No laws can create them. Only noble families can create them.

Student 1: Please explain.

Mr. Order and Control: No family can grow or survive without order and control.

Student 2: What do you mean?

Mrs. Order and Control: Where there is order—sincerity, justice, goodness, and balance—a family blooms like a familiar flower.

Student 3: What about the individual?

Mr. Order and Control: I'm pleased you asked. A well-ordered family can only be made of disciplined and organized individuals.

Student 1: Which brings us full circle to noble leaders.

Mrs. Order and Control: Yes. Their noble lives inspire and guide the people to justice and harmony.

Mr. Mean: Enough of this talk! You are all stupid baboons. Especially you, the one they call the Great Teacher.

Students 1, 2, and 3: Watch your mouth!

Buddha: Let him speak.

Mrs. Mean: Your speech is only foul-smelling air, and your wisdom stinks.

Buddha: I teach my students to return evil with kindness.

Mr. Mean: Don't play word games with us, old man. We spit on your kindness.

Students 1, 2, and 3: Great One, you need not listen to such rudeness. Let us take him away.

Buddha: Wait. I have one short question for Mr. and Mrs. Mean.

Mrs. Mean: Go ahead, old man.

Buddha: Friends, if someone offers you a gift and you do not accept it, who is its owner?

Mr. Mean: Owner of the gift? Why, the one who offered it.

Buddha: Very well. Now, since I will not accept the rudeness you offer, keep it to yourselves, and go in peace.

PROGRESS? BAH HUMBUG!

Pre-Reading Suggestions:

Prediction
✦ Have students think about what they already know of the past and brainstorm things that have evolved over the years, decades, and centuries.

Point of View
✦ Ask students if progress is positive or negative. Have them consider both sides and explain situations in which progress could be seen as both positive and negative.

Assessing Prior Knowledge
✦ Have students work in pairs or in small groups to create an impromptu list, in chronological order (from earliest through present day), of inventions related to communication.

Post-Reading Suggestions:

Vocabulary Development
✦ Lead a discussion on the difference between the words "progress" and "change." Challenge students to write paragraphs explaining the difference.

Timelines
✦ Challenge students to create a timeline that summarizes the development of communication in America. Have students determine when the timeline should begin.

Independent Research
✦ Have students research—and then compare and contrast—the communication systems we have available in our country with those found in other countries.

Prediction

◆ Encourage students to make generalizations about how they believe communication will change over the next century.

PROGRESS? BAH HUMBUG!

Note to Teacher

✦ This short skit addresses changes in communication over time in a humorous way.

✦ Have students add more parts to this Reader's Theater by researching other changes in communication.

✦ Encourage students to write a script about changes over time for some other topic, such as: housing, medicine, transportation, clothing, sports equipment, modern conveniences and appliances, manners, hobbies, architecture, entertainment, language, and conservation.

Cast of Characters

Senior Citizens 1–16
(More characters can easily be added so that every person has a speaking part.)

Setting

Senior citizens having a conversation in a retirement facility

---

Senior Citizen 1: My grandson sent me a laptop in the mail.

Senior Citizen 2: What for?

Senior Citizen 1: So I can blog.

Senior Citizen 3: What's blogging?

Senior Citizen 4: That's the way kids talk to each other these days.

Senior Citizen 1: No, that's e-mail. Blogging is newer. Blog is short for web log, and a blog is basically an online journal that you share with the world.

Senior Citizen 5: Sounds like the telegraph system to me. We had that when I was a young boy. Never used it much after we got the telephone.

Senior Citizen 2: Doesn't your grandson have a telephone?

Senior Citizen 1: Of course he does. He has a cell phone.

Senior Citizen 6: I have one of those. My kids sent me a fancy little cell phone so I could talk to them any time I wanted.

Senior Citizen 7: Yeah, my granddaughter sent me one of those things, but it's so small that I can't read the numbers. What was wrong with dialing the number the old rotary way? I don't like these newfangled push buttons!

Senior Citizen 8: I know what you mean. My kids sent me one, too. It is so small that I can't find it most of the time, and when I do find it, the charge has run down.

Senior Citizen 9: What was wrong with the phone on the wall that you cranked? And then you told the operator, a real person, who you wanted to contact. The operator would even tell you who was new in town and who was sick.

Senior Citizen 10: What's so dang important that you have to talk to people all the time?

Senior Citizen 11: When I was a girl, we didn't even have a crank phone. We wrote letters. We actually used pens and paper, and it was fun to wait for a reply.

Senior Citizen 12: I haven't gotten a letter in years. I think people have forgotten how to write.

Senior Citizen 13: We lived so far from town that we could only get our mail once a week if we were lucky.

Senior Citizen 14: Yeah, I remember getting news about family that was outdated before we got it.

Senior Citizen 15: Those were the days. Peace and quiet. Who needs this so-called progress?

Senior Citizen 1: Well, suit yourselves. I'm off to play video games with the grandkids. They just got a new one I really like—fitness bowling!

Senior Citizen 16: What's fitness bowling? What's a video game?

Senior Citizen 1: (*frustrated*) You probably wouldn't understand it.

Penny for Your Thoughts . . .

Communication has come a long way since the Pony Express. Imagine you are living in the year 2306. How do you think people will be communicating with each other by then?

Act 2

ADAPTATIONS

ADAPTATIONS

Introduction

In literature, *to adapt* a work means to change it from its original form. Many movies that are popular today originated as novels, folk tales, and even comic books.

When a piece of literature is changed or adapted to another form, positive and/or negative comparisons can be made to the original version.

In the first example, Kathy Mandry and Joe Toto's book *How Does It Feel to Live Next Door to a Giraffe?* is made into a play, with the lines taken directly from the original text. Changes can be made to increase or decrease the impact of the story. Have students explain how this story can help illustrate a need for tolerance.

The second adaptation takes just the moral from Aesop's fable about the tortoise and the hare (the concept that slow and steady wins the race) and adapts the story to a more modern and relevant setting.

"Anansi and the Greedy Lion" is an African folk tale. Students might want to research other African folk tales and write adaptations for them.

The last example, "Why the Hippo Has a Stubby Tail," is a pourquoi tale. This genre explains how things in nature came to be (e.g., why the sea is salty, why rabbits have long ears, and why babies say "goo"). These tales are not meant to be scientific explanations, but rather purely imaginative stories passed down from generation to generation. Challenge your students to create their own pourquoi tales.

Have students compare and contrast these adaptations with their original versions. After completion of this section of *Reader's Theater*, have students select a book, fairytale, or fable to adapt into a script. You may want to use the rubric at the back of the book to help guide students.

HOW DOES IT FEEL TO LIVE NEXT DOOR TO A GIRAFFE?

Pre-Reading Suggestions:

Prediction

◆ Have students discuss what a play entitled "How Does It Feel to Live Next Door to a Giraffe?" could be about.

Assessing Prior Knowledge

◆ Explain that this play takes place in a zoo. Ask students to brainstorm the kinds of animals that might be found in a zoo and the special needs all of these animals might have.

Vocabulary Development

◆ Have students define, and share examples of, tolerance.

Post-Reading Suggestions:

Reading Comprehension

◆ Ask students what lesson they think the author wanted them to get from reading this play. How can they apply this lesson in their own lives?

Research

◆ Tell students that zoos have changed during the past 200 years. Have them research these changes and make visual displays that illustrate the differences.

Expressing Ideas in Writing

◆ Have students explain how they would redesign the zoo in this Reader's Theater to make conditions better for the animals. Challenge them to further explain whether they think their changes would solve the problems.

◆ Have students write a dialogue between a grandfather gorilla and his grandchild about how things were in the "good old days" before zoos were more attuned to conservation. Were these days really "good"?

HOW DOES IT FEEL TO LIVE NEXT DOOR TO A GIRAFFE?

Note to Teacher

✦ This Reader's Theater is adapted from a book entitled *How Does It Feel to Live Next Door to a Giraffe?* by Kathy Mandry and Joe Toto, published in 1973.

Cast of Characters

Narrator	Rhino
Yak	Monkey
Giraffe	Hippo
Crocodile	Gorilla
Elephant	Fox
Leopard	Owl
Lion	Snake
Camel	Penguin
Hyena	Skunk

Setting

Zoo

Optional Props

Cardboard bars to look like cages in a zoo

Narrator: Almost everyone has a next door neighbor. You do and your friends do. Even the animals at the zoo have neighbors. They live very close to each other. Do you think you'd like that? How do you think the animals feel? Let's find out. Let's ask the yak how he feels about living next door to the giraffe.

Yak: The giraffe? Don't make me laugh. I call him The Neck. He's always sticking his big neck in here to steal my food. If I turn my head, my lunch is gone. If I take a little nap, there goes my dinner! I get skinnier and skinnier every day while The Neck gets fatter and fatter.

Giraffe: Don't listen to that yak. He pushes his fur into my cage. It makes me sneeze a lot. Don't think it's so easy for a giraffe to sneeze. A-ch-ch-ch-ch-oo-oo-oo! If I must have a neighbor, let it be the elephant. He has good manners.

Crocodile: Good manners?! He blows peanut shells in my water all day. How would you like to swim in peanut shells? They get stuck in my teeth. Just look at this mess!

Elephant: That crocodile is not my idea of a good neighbor. He's always making waves and sneaking up on me. His teeth look funny to me, too. I think he should see a dentist. If I must have a neighbor, I'd like to live near the lion. He's the king of beasts.

Leopard: The lion? He sure doesn't seem like a king to me! He keeps telling me to go to a dry cleaner. He thinks I should have my spots removed. Well, he needs a haircut! And that's not all: His roar makes my ears feel fuzzy. (*shakes head*)

Lion: That leopard is too nervous. He paces back and forth in his cage. Back and forth. Back and forth. At least try forth and back for a change! How would you like to see moving spots in front of your eyes all day? To live next to him, you need to wear a pair of sunglasses. If I must have a neighbor, give me one with a sense of humor. The hyena!

Camel: You want to live next door to Laughing Boy? Do you think you'd like to be laughed at all day? He even laughs at night, in his sleep. If I'm sick, he laughs. If I yawn, he laughs. When I eat, he laughs. He even pokes fun at the way that I look. It's no fun to be laughed at all the time.

Hyena: Hee! Hee! Hee! I have low self-esteem. It's how I deal. That camel can't take a joke. He's too serious. Hee! Hee! All he talks about are the long, hot days in the desert. Hee! Hee! And how long he can go without water. Hee! Hee! I want someone to laugh with and make me feel special. If I must have a neighbor, let it be the monkey. He'd be a lot of fun! Hee! Hee!

Rhinoceros: Fun? Do you know what he does for fun? He throws banana peels in my cage and watches me slip and fall. I guess I should consider myself lucky, though. I talked to the guy who used to live here. I don't even want to tell you what the monkey used to throw at him! It took a professional a week to clean it up.

Monkey: That rhinoceros is so clumsy! He's always banging into my cage. He makes everything shake so much that I fall out of my swing. I wish I had a big brother around. He'd take care of me. If I must have a neighbor, let it be the gorilla.

Hippopotamus: Some big brother! All he does is play in his rubber tire. He thinks he's smart because he can do things with his opposable thumbs. If he beats his chest one more time, I think I'll bellow!

Gorilla: That hippopotamus is an old mudball! He wallows in mud all day. He splashes it in my cage! Then he opens his big mouth and bellows at me. He sounds like a sick tuba. If I must have a neighbor, let it be the owl. He's smart.

Fox: I wanted someone I could talk to. But all the owl ever says is, "Whooo." If I ask him a question, he says, "Whooo." He even says, "Whooo" all night long when nobody is listening. I've been trying to teach him to at least say, "Whom." That would be different.

Owl: You have to watch a fox. He's sneaky. Did you know that he raided henhouses as a youth? That's right! He has a record. And that's not all. He never stops talking. He's always bothering me with his foolish words. With a neighbor like that, I'm lucky to get in a "Whooo" once in a while. If I must have a neighbor, let it be the penguin. Everything is black and white with him.

Rattlesnake: That penguin thinks he's so important because he's dressed in a tuxedo and he was in a movie. Mr. Hollywood, walking with his nose in the air. Who wants to live near him? I'm more down to earth.

Penguin: I don't like any snakes, especially not that one. He's always hissing and striking out at me. HISS. HISS. HISSSS. He has beady eyes, too. I don't trust him. If I had my way, I wouldn't have a neighbor.

Skunk: I hear everybody complaining about their neighbors. I get very lonely living by myself. I'd like to live next door to some-one—anyone at all. Hello? Anyone?

Penny for Your Thoughts . . .

Imagine you had to live in the zoo on display for all to see. Write a narrative entitled, "A Day in the Life of Me." The setting is in a zoo cage. What are your feelings?

THE TORTOISE
AND THE HARE

Pre-Reading Suggestions:

Vocabulary Development
✦ Have students define adaptation as it applies in literature.

Assessing Prior Knowledge
✦ Ask students to retell and then summarize the well-known Aesop's fable "The Tortoise and the Hare." Have students discuss the moral or lesson illustrated in this fable.

Prediction
✦ Tell students that the lesson from this famous tale has been used in a modern-day version with people instead of animals. Ask them to predict what the scenario might be.

Post-Reading Suggestions:

Comparing and Contrasting
✦ Ask students how they think this adaptation is the same and different when compared to "The Tortoise and the Hare."

Expressing Ideas in Writing
✦ Tell the class to think back on the play and write to answer the following question: Which student do you identify with most, and why?
✦ Tell students to imagine that this story has just come out in a story collection book in the library, and that they were asked to write a critique for the school newspaper. Ask the following questions: How would you describe the story? Would you give it a thumbs-up or a thumbs-down? Why?

Research

✦ Challenge students to go to the library and see how many adaptations they can find of some of their favorite fairytales, folk tales, fables, and classics. Have students select an adaptation they like better than the original and share it with the class.

THE TORTOISE AND THE HARE

Note to Teacher

✦ This is an adaptation of "The Tortoise and the Hare." In Aesop's version of this famous fable, all of the characters are animals.

Cast of Characters

Student 1	Student 4
Student 2	Student 5
Student 3	Teacher

Setting

A classroom where students are sitting and waiting for the teacher to arrive

Optional Props

6 chairs in classroom configuration

1 teacher's desk

Student 1: I am going to finish this test so fast. I'm going to have it done before you can put your name on yours.

Student 2: We have a test?

Student 3: Yes we do—every Friday. And every Friday you forget.

Student 2: Well, at least I remember to forget.

Student 4: (*nervously*) This test is life or death. If I don't pass, I'll never be an astronaut.

Student 3: You have never earned less than an "A." You're the smartest person I have ever met, and I've met a lot of people.

Student 4: Thanks. But all those good grades could have been a fluke, a mere flash in the pan, an oasis in the middle of a desert . . .

Student 1: Whatever! I'm going to finish first and be on the bus sitting by the window.

Student 5: So what if you get to sit next to the window? You've been in the same grade for 2 years.

Student 1: Yeah, but I always sit next to the window. Look at my tan. Just look at it!

Student 5: Well, it is nice, don't get me wrong—even though everyone knows by now how damaging the sun's rays can be to the skin. I just think you should take your time, read carefully, and think about the answers.

Student 2: Teacher! Hide! Wait, never mind, don't hide. We're supposed to be here.

Teacher: (*entering the room*) OK, class, we have a test. Take out your pencils and put away your things.

Student 2: (*raises hand*)

Teacher: Yes, we have a test.

Student 2: (*puts hand down*)

Student 1: I'm going to finish first!

Teacher: Please take your time. I like you, but having you in my class for 2 years in a row is enough. I think 3 years would be pushing it.

Student 3: Can I pass out the tests?

Teacher: Yes, you may, but no extra points.

Student 3: Well, I guess I'll still do it. (*passes out the test*)

Student 1: Finished! Done! Have a good day!

Teacher: Are you sure you're finished?

Student 1: Well, of course. I'm the fastest. (*hands teacher test and starts to go*)

Teacher: You don't have permission to leave. I've decided to let the person with the highest score go first today.

Student 1: What? No way! What about my tan and my perfect window sitting record? You have to let me go. (*pleading*)

Teacher: I'm sorry. You have to take your time and do things right the first time.

Student 2: We're all finished.

Teacher: Thank you. (*starts grading papers*) All right, you all got an "A"—except one of you. (*points at Student 1*) You got the worst score I have ever seen. You even got your name wrong!

Student 1: My record of sitting by the window. My perfect tan. (*leaves room hanging head and mumbling to self*)

Teacher: See you next year.

The moral of the story: Slow and steady wins the race.

ANANSI AND THE GREEDY LION

Pre-Reading Suggestions:

Vocabulary Development
◆ Have students define "greedy."
◆ Have students recall situations in which they thought someone acted greedy.

Assessing Prior Knowledge
◆ Ask students what they know about African folk tales featuring a character named Anansi. Ask them to define "trickster."
◆ Have students find examples in the library of other trickster stories, like Brer Rabbit in American folk tales, Renart the Fox in French folk tales, and Kokopelli and Coyote in Native American folk tales.

Post-Reading Suggestions:

Vocabulary Development
◆ Have students reread the play and add onomatopoeia to make it more interesting.

Expressing Ideas in Writing
◆ Have students add another scene to the play using the same characters.
◆ Have students add characters to the play.
◆ Have students work in small groups to rewrite the ending of the play, then have them share their new endings with the class.

Drawing Conclusions
◆ Ask students what they think of Anansi. Would they like to have a friend who was a trickster? Have them explain their answers.

Research
◆ Have students find the names of tricksters in folk tales from around the world.

ANANSI AND THE GREEDY LION

Note to Teacher
◆ This story is from the Ashanti legend of "Anansi the Spider" and was first told long ago in the West African country now called Ghana. Its central character is Kwaku Anansi, the heroic trickster "spider-man" who is a central figure in many West African stories.

Cast of Characters
Hare
Anansi (a spider)
Lion

Setting
Jungle

Optional Props
Students could perform this as a shadow play, creating a different shadow shape for each character. Use an overhead projector as the light source.

Hare: (*running up to Anansi*) Kwaku Anansi, His Majesty commands our presence right away. Let's hurry up and go, or he will be angry.

Anansi: What is your command, Majesty? In what way can we, small creatures that we are, be of use to the King of Beasts?

Lion: I am going on a hunt, and I want you to accompany me. They tell me that you, Kwaku Anansi, are clever, and I shall rely on you and your friend, Hare, to help me in the hunt.

Anansi: Certainly, I am clever, and I will endeavor to do my best. But I am only a small creature, so you must not expect too much.

Lion: We will leave at once. (*they walk around as if through the jungle and come to a stop*)

Hare: Game is plentiful here, even though the bush is thick.

Lion: (*sitting down*) Now you can tell me the easiest way to catch animals, for I am tired and cannot be bothered to show my strength.

Anansi: I am only a poor creature, of course, Your Majesty, but indeed, I have a suggestion to make.

Lion: Say on.

Anansi: Well, Your Majesty, I suggest that we dig many pits and cover them with vines. Then Your Majesty should walk around the area, roaring. This will cause confusion, and all of the animals, thinking you are after them, will run hither and thither and fall into the pits.

Lion: An excellent idea. You may dig the pits while I sleep.

(*Anansi and Hare make movements as if digging pits*)

Hare: (*loudly*) The pits are ready, Your Majesty.

Lion: (*stretches and walks on stage, roaring*)

Hare: (*to spider*) The animals heard the Lion and they are frightened. They have run from their lairs and dens. They are running helter-skelter through the jungle. Many of them are falling into the pits. Look—some of them are killed already, and others are terrified.

Lion: (*comes back to check on the pits, is very satisfied with the catch*) Kwaku Anansi, your idea was indeed a good one. Let me congratulate you. There remains only the question of taking the meat home. Kwaku Anansi, how do you intend to do this?

Anansi: That is easy, Your Majesty. The Hare and I have built a sled of branches. All we have to do is pile the meat on the sled, and you can pull the meat home.

Hare: Yes, the sled is ready, Your Majesty.

Lion: So it is. But I've been thinking, and I think it would be a better idea for the two of you to pull the sled, because there are two of you and only one of me. (**Hare nods in agreement**)

Anansi: Your Majesty, it is not fitting, nor is it possible, for small animals such as ourselves to draw the magnificent catch of His Majesty the Lion. If Your Majesty draws the sled, then everyone will know that the catch is indeed yours.

(Lion nods yes, Hare and Anansi put strap of sled over Lion's body, and all three take three steps in unison to the first pit, three steps to the second pit, and so on)

Hare: We are at the Lion's lair.

Lion: (*not wanting to share the meat*) Hare, what do you think we should do with the meat?

Hare: (*stuttering and nervous*) W-w-well, Your Majesty, who am I to presume to tell the King of Beasts what to do with his own meat? But, at any time, should Your Majesty feel like giving me a little bit, I shall be more than grateful.

Lion: (*very pleased*) Very well, Hare. When I have eaten, you shall have a bit of what remains. Now, Kwaku Anansi, what about you?

Anansi: (*very hungry, and knowing he has done most of the work, replies boldly*) Well, Your Majesty, since you have asked me, I feel that since the Hare and I did much of the work, you should give us the little we need to satisfy our hunger and reserve the major part for yourself.

Lion: (*very angry*) What? Kwaku Anansi, do you presume to dictate to me, the King of the Beasts, what I should do with my own meat? It was sufficient honor that I took you with me on the hunt and showed you how to catch meat. Do you presume to demand a share of my meat? (**Lion prepares to jump on Anansi**)

Anansi: (*seeing his mistake, jumps back*) Oh no, no, Your Majesty. I require nothing. Indeed, I was not thinking of what I was saying. I beg your pardon.

Lion: (*somewhat pacified*) Kwaku Anansi, I remember now that we forgot to clear one of the pits in the forest. As punishment for your presumption, you shall go back and bring me back whatever has fallen into the trap.

Anansi: (*talking to self*) If I take more meat back to His Majesty, he may try to kill me. It is better that I think of a plan to protect myself and punish him for his greed.

Lion: You know, Hare, that Anansi is too demanding. I can't trust him. When he comes back, I am going to kill him.

Hare: I think you are right, Your Majesty. He must be killed.

Anansi: Ah ha! Here is a plant that is poisonous. I will take some of the leaves and give them to the animal that is in the pit. This will make the meat poisonous for the Lion. He will eat the meat and die. Good, there is a little monkey in the pit. (*feeds the monkey the poisonous plant and then brings it to the Lion, singing a song as he brings the meat*) Here indeed is meat fit for a King. This is the best meat in the forest. Only a King should eat it.

(*Lion hears Anansi, runs to him, grabs the meat, and gobbles it down, remembering to throw a small piece to the Hare*)

(*continues to gobble*)

(*as soon as the Lion finishes, he takes a few steps, as if to pounce on Anansi, but suddenly grabs his stomach, falls down, and begins to moan*)

Hare: (*realizing what is happening to the Lion, runs over to Anansi, pleading*) Oh, Anansi, please have pity on me. I beg your forgiveness for siding with the Lion. Please don't let me die! Don't kill me like you did the Lion!

Anansi: You only ate a little of the meat, Hare, so you will be all right in a couple of days. I didn't kill the Lion—he killed himself with his own greed.

WHY THE HIPPO HAS A STUBBY TAIL

Pre-Reading Suggestions:

Assessing Prior Knowledge

✦ Have students describe what a hippo looks like.

✦ Have students brainstorm all they know about hippos.

Vocabulary Development

✦ Introduce the word "porquoi" and have students brainstorm examples.

Post-Reading Suggestions:

Literary Response

✦ Have students retell and then summarize the story.

Expressing Ideas in Writing

✦ Students may work in pairs or in small groups to write an original pourquoi story.

Research

✦ Challenge students to go to the library and see how many pourquoi stories they can find.

WHY THE HIPPO HAS A STUBBY TAIL

Note to Teacher

✦ "Why the Hippo Has a Stubby Tail" is a porquoi tale. This genre explains how things in nature came to be. These tales are not meant to be scientific explanations, but rather purely imaginative stories.

Cast of Characters
Hare
Elephant
Narrator
Hippo

Setting
Jungle

Optional Props
Rope

Hare: (*Hare takes a long rope over to Elephant*) Elephant, today I want to show you that I am stronger than you. Let's pull each other by means of this rope.

Elephant: (*laughing*) Who are you, little Hare, to think of such a thing?

Hare: I know that I am smaller than you, but I know that I am strong. Come! Here's the rope. I'm going to show you now.

Elephant: (*laughing*) I don't believe this, but go ahead.

Hare: You see, you are going to stand here at the top end, and I will go and stand at the bottom end, on the bank of the river. Take hold of this end of the rope, but you are not to pull until I give you the signal. I am going to hold the other end of the rope. When I get to the bank of the river, I'll tug the rope twice. When you feel the rope go tug, tug, then begin to pull.

Narrator: Then the Hare took hold of his end of the rope and ran to the bank of the river. When he got there, he called out to the Hippo.

Hare: Hippo! Hippo! Where are you?

Hippo: (*surfacing from the water*) I am here.

Hare: You think you are a very strong animal. But today, I want to show that even though you are big, you are not as strong as I am. Just take hold of this end of the rope. I am going to the other end up there, and you and I are going to pull each other.

Hippo: (*laughing heartily*) This is so funny. But if you insist, I will do as you say.

Hare: You are going to stand here in the water and hold this end until I give you the signal to pull. When the rope goes tug, tug, you had better pull with all your might and strength.

Narrator: Then the Hare went to the center of the rope and tugged it twice. Immediately, the Elephant pulled at the top end, and the Hippo pulled at the bottom end. The Hare sat down in the shade and watched. They pulled and pulled. They couldn't believe that the Hare was so strong. The Elephant began to think that the Hare had some help.

Elephant: What?! Is the Hare so strong, then? Can it be that he has asked some other animals to help him? Well, if he has, I'll soon find out.

Narrator: Then the Elephant pulled even harder. The Hippo was suspicious, too, and he used all his strength and pulled and pulled. But very soon, he found himself being pulled right out of the water. He was shocked!

Hippo: Pulled out of my place by the Hare! I am sure he is not alone. But I'll have to stop pulling until we come face to face. And if I find that he is tricking me, I'll deal with him!

Narrator: The pulling went on and on, and the Elephant, who never shifted from his original position, brought the Hippo nearer and nearer, and the coils of rope heaped higher and higher in front of the Elephant. At last, the Hippo lost all his strength and found himself being drawn faster and faster—until he came face to face with the Elephant! Both of them were startled to see each other.

Elephant: Oh! So it's you! You tricked me into this in order to try my strength.

Hippo: Mercy, oh Great One! I didn't know that I was pulling against you. The Hare challenged me to pull, and all this time, I thought I was pulling him.

Elephant: (*indignant*) You thought you were pulling the Hare? Do you understand what you are saying?

Hippo: Believe me, Great One. In truth, I now know that I was pulling you, but the Hare said to me that he would hold the other end. In fact, I myself was wondering where he got so much strength.

Elephant: Do you think I'm going to believe that tale? I'll not be tricked a second time. What is more, I'm going to teach you a lesson. Choose between two fates: that I kill you, or that I cut off your tail!

Hippo: Oh Great One! I implore you neither to kill me nor to cut off my tail. Believe me when I say that—

Narrator: But the Elephant would listen no longer. Instead, he pulled out a sharp, crude knife and took long strides toward the Hippo. Seeing this, the Hippo turned quickly to run away. But the Elephant sprang forward, caught him by the tail, and chopped it off!

Hippo: Oh! How can I return to my family in such disgrace, without my tail?

Narrator: The Hippo was so ashamed that he hung his head and walked slowly back to the river. But by the time he got there, he'd had a brilliant idea!

Hippo: All hippos assemble! All hippos assemble! I decree that from this day forward, all hippos must cut off their tails.

Narrator: This decree was carried out, and so it is to this very day that all hippos have stubby tails.

Act 3

FORMAT MODELS

FORMAT MODELS

Introduction

In the following section, students will be introduced to a variety of formats they can use as models to create their own scripts.

In "Time Travel," have students imagine they are traveling in a time machine. Tell them they can set the date for their time machine to any event in history. They are to research the event and then write a script as if they were actually witnessing the event unfold. Before the class makes their presentations, have students create a time machine built for two using boxes, recyclables, plastic piping, and lots of imagination.

The next three examples are modeled after a retro 1950s television game show, **To Tell the Truth**. Each of the three contestants claims to be the same person. The panelists (the rest of the class) have to determine which one of the three contestants is telling the truth. After researching a historic figure, students should create a script.

The last three models are examples of choral readings. The first is a fairytale choral reading that pokes fun at fairytale stereotypes. The second and third models are about real periods in history. One is set during a time when many people fled to America for freedom; the other is about one of America's favorite holidays, Thanksgiving.

TIME TRAVEL

Cast of Characters
Time Traveler 1
Time Traveler 2

Settings on Time Machine
Date: 1933
Place: Toll House Inn, Whitman, MA
Event: the serendipitous discovery of chocolate chip cookies

Optional Props
Time machine made in class
Toll House cookies students can enjoy after the Reader's Theater

---

Time Traveler 1 (TT1): I'm going to surprise you today by setting the time machine to a date and place that I don't think you will recognize.

Time Traveler 2 (TT2): I'm pretty good at history. I'll bet I can guess.

TT1: I know you are really good at history—that's why we are going to do something different.

TT2: How different?

TT1: Well, I can't say that this event changed life as we know it. It was more of an invention or discovery.

TT2: I love inventions. They are historical. Imagine where we would be without them.

TT1: Do you know what a serendipitous discovery is?

TT2: Sure, something that is discovered purely by accident.

TT1: That's right. OK, buckle up. Here we go!

TT2: We are in a kitchen. There are many inventions in here.

TT1: To be exact, we are in the kitchen of Mrs. Ruth Wakefield. She and her husband run this travel lodge, called the Toll House Inn, here in Whitman, Massachusetts.

TT2: Hmm, doesn't ring a bell. What is she doing?

TT1: Mrs. Wakefield is known for her delicious desserts. She is trying to mix up a batch of chocolate drop cookies.

TT2: That's interesting, but I can't imagine what famous discovery will come from that.

TT1: See how she is looking a little flustered? She's looking through all her cabinets.

TT2: Yes, she seems pretty unhappy.

TT1: Keep watching. This is when it gets interesting.

TT2: She seems to have found something. It looks like a chocolate candy bar.

TT1: It is. You see, the recipe she is using—her favorite recipe—calls for a special kind of chocolate called baker's chocolate. She didn't realize she had run out of that ingredient until it was too late.

TT2: What is she doing to the candy bar?

TT1: She's chopping it into small pieces in hopes that it will blend into the cookie dough, like baker's chocolate would.

TT2: You mean it didn't?

TT1: Nope. The chocolate bits softened, but they didn't melt enough to blend.

TT2: Wait a minute. I think I get it now.

TT1: What do you think she discovered?

TT2: My favorite—chocolate chip cookies.

TT1: You are right. Her cookies became so popular that people came from miles around to buy them. People just couldn't get enough chocolate chip cookies.

TT2: So I'll bet the sales of chocolate went off the charts after that.

TT1: Right again. As a matter of fact, the sales were so good that the owner of a famous chocolate company struck a deal with Mrs. Wakefield. They would print the recipe for her cookies on their chocolate products, and she would get a lifetime supply of free chocolate chips.

TT2: A lifetime supply of chocolate. WOW! (*pauses*) Wait a minute. You said the name of their inn was Toll House?

TT1: That's right. The house was originally built in 1709 as a place where weary travelers could rest, change horses, pay their toll taxes, and get a home-cooked meal.

TT2: And the recipe printed on the packages of chocolate was for Toll House cookies?

TT1: That right. There are dozens of variations on the original Toll House cookie Mrs. Wakefield discovered, but she gets all the credit.

TT2: I wish I could serendipitously discover something.

TT1: Who knows? One day you might.

TT2: Let's go back. For some reason, I'm in the mood for chocolate!

TO TELL THE TRUTH: J. K. ROWLING

Cast of Characters

Narrator or Teacher

Game Show Host

J. K. Rowling 1

J. K. Rowling 2

J. K. Rowling 3

Setting

A game show

Optional Props

3 chairs

Narrator or Teacher: Today we are going to play a game called "To Tell The Truth." Each of three contestants will claim to be J. K. Rowling, the author of the award-winning *Harry Potter* series. The panelists (that's all of you) will guess which one of the three contestants is telling the truth. Take a minute now to write the numbers 1 through 5. When I read a question, listen carefully to the answers from the three contestants. The phony claimants could lie or exaggerate the truth, but the real J. K. Rowling has to tell the truth when questioned. At the conclusion of the show, I will say, "Will the real J. K. Rowling please stand up or step forward?" and you will see if you were correct.

Game Show Host (GSH): Hello, contestants. Will you please identify yourselves?

J. K. Rowling 1 (JKR 1): I am J. K. Rowling.

J. K. Rowling 2 (JKR 2): I am J. K. Rowling.

J. K. Rowling 3 (JKR 3): I am J. K. Rowling.

GSH: (*to audience*) Only one of these contestants is J. K. Rowling. It is your job to listen carefully to the answers each one gives to the questions that I pose. The real J. K. Rowling will always tell the truth. You are welcome to take notes during the questioning so you can eliminate the imposters by the end of the game.

GSH: Question #1: What was the original title of your first Harry Potter book?

JKR 1: *Harry Potter and the Wizard.*

JKR 2: *The Adventures of Harry Potter.*

JKR 3: *Harry Potter and the Philosopher's Stone.*

GSH: Question #2: What is something most of your fans don't know about you?

JKR 1: I write all of my novels on a laptop computer.

JKR 2: That my real name is Elizabeth. I just made up the initials to sound more mysterious.

JKR 3: My first book was called **Rabbit**, and I wrote it when I was 6.

GSH: Question #3: Where did you get the money to quit your regular job and finish writing your book?

JKR 1: I sold my car and several pieces of jewelry.

JKR 2: I borrowed the money from a dear friend who believed in me.

JKR 3: I received a grant from the Scottish Arts Council.

GSH: Question #4: Where did you come up with the name Harry Potter?

JKR 1: I just made it up. I liked the sound of it.

JKR 2: I had a dream, and when I woke up, I could see Harry Potter's face, and the name just came to me.

JKR 3: When I was little, I lived next door to a family named Potter, and I never forgot the children or their names.

GSH: Question #5: When and where were you born?

JKR 1: I was born on July 31, 1955, in Ireland.

JKR 2: I was born on July 31, 1975, in Wales.

JKR 3: I was born on July 31, 1965, in England.

GSH: (*to audience*) Take a few minutes to decide who you think is the real J. K. Rowling. Is it #1, #2, or #3? (*have students write their selections on note cards or in journals*)

GSH: Will the real J. K. Rowling please stand up or step forward? (*after a little teasing, #3 stands up*)

NOTE: Have students discuss clues that helped them make the correct choice. Review the answers from Contestant #3 so there are no misunderstandings.

TO TELL THE TRUTH: HARRIET TUBMAN

Cast of Characters

Narrator or Teacher

Game Show Host

Harriet Tubman 1

Harriet Tubman 2

Harriet Tubman 3

Setting

A game show

Optional Props

3 chairs

Narrator or Teacher: Today we are going to play a game called "To Tell The Truth." Each of three contestants will claim to be Harriet Tubman, one of the most important African American abolitionists and inspirational women in United States history. The panelists (that's all of you) will guess which one of the three contestants is telling the truth. Take a minute now to write the numbers 1 through 6. When I read a question, listen carefully to the answers from the three contestants. The phony claimants could lie or exaggerate the truth, but the real Harriet Tubman has to tell the truth when questioned. At the conclusion of the show, I will say, "Will the real Harriet Tubman please stand up or step forward?" and you will see if you were correct.

Game Show Host (GSH): Hello, contestants. Will you please identify yourselves?

Harriet Tubman 1 (HT 1): I am Harriet Tubman.

Harriet Tubman 2 (HT 2): I am Harriet Tubman.

Harriet Tubman 3 (HT 3): I am Harriet Tubman.

GSH: (*to audience*) Only one of these contestants is Harriet Tubman. It is your job to listen carefully to the answers each one gives to the questions that I pose. The real Harriet Tubman will always tell the truth. You are welcome to take notes during the questioning so you can eliminate the imposters by the end of the game.

GSH: Question #1: When and where were you born?

HT 1: I was born in 1830 in Africa.

HT 2: I was born in 1820 in the U.S.

HT 3: I was born in 1820 in New York.

GSH: Question #2: You first proved you were brave when you did what?

HT 1: I helped slaves run away on the Underground Railroad.

HT 2: I refused to help the plantation overseer stop a slave from running away.

HT 3: I jumped on a runaway horse that was heading toward slaves in the field.

GSH: Question #3: An angry overseer threw a heavy rock at a slave, but the rock hit you instead. Where did it hit you?

HT 1: I was hit in the back, on my spine. I always had a slight limp after that.

HT 2: I was hit in the head. I suffered from blackouts for the rest of my life.

HT 3: I was hit on the shoulder. I was never able to reach as high after that.

GSH: Question #4: You escaped to freedom with the help of the Underground Railroad. Why did you continually risk your life and freedom to go back to guide others to safety?

HT 1: I was paid well and needed the money.

HT 2: I felt that my family and friends should be able to enjoy freedom as much as I did.

HT 3: I have always been a risk taker, and I enjoyed the excitement.

GSH: Question #5: History says you were sometimes known as "Moses." How did you get that nickname?

HT 1: I often read from the Bible for inspiration.

HT 2: Moses led slaves to freedom hundreds of years ago, just as I led slaves to freedom.

HT 3: I needed a code name, so I used Moses.

GSH: Question #6: Besides your brave involvement with the Underground Railroad, what other accomplishment are you most proud of?

HT 1: I was the first Black woman to serve in the U.S. Senate.

HT 2: I donated land for the purpose of building a home for sick and needy Black people.

HT 3: I worked hard to give women the right to vote.

GSH: (*to audience*) Take a few minutes to decide who you think is the real Harriet Tubman. Is it #1, #2, or #3? (**have students write their selections on note cards or in journals**)

GSH: Will the real Harriet Tubman please stand up or step forward? (**after a little teasing, #2 stands up**)

NOTE: Have students discuss clues that helped them make the correct choice. Review the answers from Contestant #2 so there are no misunderstandings or misconceptions.

TO TELL THE TRUTH: LEWIS AND CLARK

Cast of Characters
Narrator or Teacher
Game Show Host
Lewis and Clark 1
Lewis and Clark 2
Lewis and Clark 3

Setting
On a game show

Optional Props
6 chairs

Narrator or Teacher: Today we are going to play a game called "To Tell the Truth." Each of three contestant pairs will claim to be Meriwether Lewis and William Clark, the famous explorers. The panelists (that's all of you) will guess which one of the three contestant pairs is telling the truth. Take a minute now to write the numbers 1 through 8. When I read a question, listen carefully to the answers from the contestants. The phony claimants could lie or exaggerate the truth, but the real Lewis and Clark will always tell the truth when questioned. At the conclusion of the show, I will say, "Will the real Lewis and Clark please stand up or step forward?" and you will see if you were correct.

Game Show Host (GSH): Hello, contestants. Will you please identify yourselves?

Meriwether Lewis 1 (ML 1): I am Meriwether Lewis, and he (*points to partner*) is William Clark.

Meriwether Lewis 2 (ML 2): I am Meriwether Lewis, and he (*points to partner*) is William Clark.

Meriwether Lewis 3 (ML 3): I am Meriwether Lewis, and he (*points to partner*) is William Clark.

GSH: (*to audience*) Obviously, all three pairs of contestants cannot be Lewis and Clark. It is your job to listen carefully to their answers to my questions.

The real Lewis and Clark will always tell the truth. You are welcome to take notes during the questioning so you can eliminate the imposters by the end of the game. Here's Question #1: Why did you decide to explore the western rivers across North America in search of a waterway leading to a western ocean?

William Clark 1 (WC 1): President Jefferson and Congress were very interested to see what lay beyond the Mississippi River.

William Clark 2 (WC 2): I wasn't actually looking for a passage across North America. That happened by accident.

William Clark 3 (WC 3): President Tom Jefferson and I go way back. We were university roommates. He was the best man at my wedding, so naturally, when he asked me to lead an expedition, I couldn't refuse.

GSH: Now, for Question #2: What were you hoping to find along the way?

ML 1: New plants and animals unknown in the eastern part of the country.

ML 2: We were hoping to find unusual landforms and animals. We wanted to see volcanoes and woolly mammoths.

ML 3: We expected to find many friendly Indians, and we brought gifts for all of them.

GSH: OK, now here's Question #3: Where did your expedition start?

WC 1: We started at the Missouri River.

WC 2: We started at the Colorado River.

WC 3: We started at the Mississippi River.

GSH: Great answers, guys. Now, here's Question #4: Besides the Lewis and Clark Expedition, your combined journal is often referred to as what?

ML 1: The Corps of Discovery.

ML 2: Lewis's Expedition.

ML 3: The most successful expedition in the history of North America.

GSH: Here's Question #5: Mr. Clark, we all know that you spent most of your time on the keelboat, charting the course and making maps. What did Mr. Lewis do?

WC 1: Lewis was often ashore, studying the rock formations, soil, animals, and plants.

WC 2: Lewis was in charge of supplies and keeping morale up among the men.

WC 3: Lewis did most of the hunting and cooking.

GSH: Now on to Question #6: Who ended up being the most valuable member of your expedition?

ML 1: Sacagawea was the most valuable member of the expedition. She saved our lives many times along the way.

ML 2: That's easy. It was Searcy, my dog, a 150-pound Newfoundland. He was always able to help us find food, he entertained the men, and he helped us make friends with the natives.

ML 3: Mr. Toussaint Charbonneau, a French mountain man, was invaluable as a guide and interpreter.

GSH: Here's Question #7: What do you regret most about your expedition?

WC 1: That the friendly relationships we made with the Native Americans did not last.

WC 2: That I didn't make any money on this expedition and died a poor man.

WC 3: That Thomas Jefferson didn't get more credit for having such a great idea.

GSH: Here's Question #8: Why is the expedition so well known?

ML 1: Probably because we traveled the length of the Missouri River, crossed the Rocky Mountains, reached the Pacific Ocean, and came back again. Most of this journey was over completely unknown land.

ML 2: Probably because there have been so many books and movies made about it.

ML 3: Probably because Thomas Jefferson was the only president ever to organize an expedition for discovery.

GSH: (*to audience*) Well, that's it for my questions. Now take a few minutes to decide who you think are the real Lewis and Clark. Are they Lewis and Clark #1? Lewis and Clark #2? Or Lewis and Clark #3? (***have students write their selections on note cards or in journals***)

GSH: Will the real Lewis and Clark please stand up or step forward? (***after a little teasing, Lewis and Clark #1 stand up***)

NOTE: Have students discuss clues that helped them make the correct choice. Finally, reread all of the answers Lewis and Clark #1 gave in order to reinforce the correct answers.

THE EMPEROR WITH A ROTTEN ATTITUDE

Note to Teacher

◆ Assign parts for Narrators 1–10. Then have all students form five groups, and assign each group to a character below.

◆ Each group should respond with the appropriate words and expressions when their cue is given in the reading of the story. Read through the story once so students can get familiar with their cues.

◆ All students will supply the sound effects of coughing and galloping horses at the end.

Character	Response
Emperor With a Rotten Attitude	holds nose and says, "P U"
Prince Who Dropped Out of School	shrugs shoulders and says, "Whadja say?"
Prince Who Is Muscle-Bound	makes body poses and says, "Grrr"
Prince Who Is Kind, Intelligent, and Sensitive	smiles broadly, bows, and says, "How do you do?"
Princess Who Is Independent, Intelligent, and Clean, With Great Teeth	curtsies and says, "Fine, thank you, and you?"

Narrator 1: There was once an emperor with a rotten attitude (**"P U"**). He had three sons. The eldest son dropped out of school (**"Whadja say?"**).

The second son was exceedingly muscular; all he ever did was lift weights, pose, and look at himself in the mirror (**"Grrr"**).

The youngest son was kind, intelligent, and sensitive (**"How do you do?"**).

Reader's Theater for Grades 3–4 © Taylor & Francis Groups. • Permission is granted to photocopy or reproduce this page for single classroom use only.

Narrator 2: Now, in the nearby Indus Valley, there lived an independent, intelligent, and clean princess with great teeth (**"Fine, thank you, and you?"**). From birth, she had been told that there was an agreement, written in Sanskrit, that she would marry one of the emperor's sons so that their two powerful families could unite.

One day, she came to the palace of the emperor with a rotten attitude (**"P U"**). "I have come," said she, "to seek a husband among your three sons." (**"Whadja say?" "Grrr" "How do you do?"**)

Narrator 3: First she was introduced to the eldest son (**"Whadja say?"**). She tried to carry on an intelligent conversation with him about current events, but every time she would ask for his opinion, he would say (**"Whadja say?"**).

Narrator 4: Then the muscle-bound prince appeared (**"Grrr"**), but every time she tried to bring up an interesting topic for discussion, he would just pose and say (**"Grrr"**).

Narrator 5: The princess (**"Fine, thank you, and you?"**) said to the emperor (**"P U"**), "These men will not make good husbands. What about your youngest son (**"How do you do?"**)?"

This angered the emperor with a rotten attitude (**"P U"**). He said, "You cannot take my youngest son (**"How do you do?"**)!"

Narrator 6: "Well," she replied, "I cannot love your eldest son (**"Whadja say?"**), and I don't like your muscle-bound son (**"Grrr"**)."

Just then on the stairway appeared the youngest son (**"How do you do?"**), bowing courteously as he gazed upon the great teeth of the princess. The princess immediately struck up a conversation with him so they could get to know each other. The youngest son (**"How do you do?"**) appeared to be kind, intelligent, and sensitive to the feelings of the princess (**"Fine, thank you, and you?"**).

Narrator 7: Looking relieved, the princess announced, "I will take your youngest son (**"How do you do?"**) to be my husband so that the agreement between our two families can be fulfilled."

Her words angered the emperor with a rotten attitude (**"P U"**). He wanted to keep his commitment to the princess's family and knew the union would be good for his empire, but he also knew his youngest son (**"How do you do?"**) was the only one of his three sons who had any sense.

Narrator 8: "Call out the guards," he thundered, "and turn out this picky princess (**"Fine, thank you, and you?"**)!"

But the princess (**"Fine, thank you and you?"**) immediately grabbed the hand of the willing prince (**"How do you do?"**) and rushed out the door. They both leaped up onto her swift stallion and galloped off, raising dust along the way (**coughing and galloping sounds, which gradually fade away**).

Narrator 9: The prince (**"How do you do?"**) and the princess (**"Fine, thank you, and you?"**) escaped safely because her army of equally as intelligent, independent, and clean ladies-in-waiting, who all had great teeth also, stopped the emperor's men from following them. They did this not by using violence, but by using engaging, interesting, and charming conversation.

Narrator 10: So ends the romantic tale of the emperor with the rotten attitude (**"P U"**); his son who dropped out of school (**"Whadja say?"**); his muscle-bound son who posed all of the time, lifted weights, and stared at himself in the mirror (**"Grrr"**); his youngest son, who was kind, intelligent, and sensitive (**"How do you do?"**); and the independent, intelligent, and clean princess with great teeth (**"Fine, thank you, and you?"**), who had a fast-moving horse.

Penny for Your Thoughts . . .

Imagine you have been challenged to incorporate another prince into this play. Create a description of him and the phrase that would be mentioned each time the reader heard his name.

THE PEOPLE MOVED TO AMERICA!

Note to Teacher

✦ This Reader's Theater can be sung to the tune of "The Green Grass Grows All Around," or it can be read as a choral reading, where the Narrator or teacher reads the call, and the students provide the echo response.

Narrator or Teacher:
There was a king,

Students:
There was a king,

Narrator or Teacher:
Who ruled the land,

Students:
Who ruled the land,

Narrator or Teacher:
Was the meanest king,

Students:
Was the meanest king,

Narrator or Teacher:
That you ever did see!

Students:
That you ever did see!

Narrator and Students:
Well, the king was mean,
So the people moved,
To America,
To America!

Narrator or Teacher:
In America,

Students:
In America,

Narrator or Teacher:
We have some rights,

Students:
We have some rights,

Narrator or Teacher:
That are given to us,

Students:
That are given to us,

Narrator or Teacher:
By the Constitution!

Students:
By the Constitution!

Narrator and Students:
Well, we have some rights,
'Cause the king was mean,
And the people moved,
To America,
To America!

Narrator or Teacher:
In America,

Students:
In America,

Narrator or Teacher:
The people choose,

Students:

The people choose,

Narrator or Teacher:

The president,

Students:

The president,

Narrator or Teacher:

And others, too!

Students:

And others, too!

Narrator and Students:

Well, the people choose,
And they have some rights,
'Cause the king was mean,
And the people moved,
To America,
To America!

Narrator or Teacher:

In America,

Students:

In America,

Narrator or Teacher:

We follow laws,

Students:

We follow laws,

Narrator or Teacher:

That protect our things,

Students:

That protect our things,

Narrator or Teacher:
And keep us safe from harm!

Students:
And keep us safe from harm!

Narrator and Students:
Well, we follow laws,
And the people choose,
And we have some rights,
'Cause the king was mean,
And the people moved,
To America,
To America!

Penny for Your Thoughts . . .

What other rights, laws, and freedoms do we enjoy as Americans? Write three new verses to this song telling about them.

GIVE THANKS TO THE PILGRIMS

Note to Teacher

✦ There are 13 speaking parts for colonists, and after each colonist reads, the rest of the class should read the corresponding refrain.

PART 1

FIRST COLONIST:

We are the Pilgrims who seek a new home.
We are going to the New World to worship in our own way.
We are sailing toward the free New World.

PART 1 REFRAIN: (repeat after each of the following stanzas)

The winds, how they blew!
The storms, how they raged!
But the ship sailed on and on.

SECOND COLONIST:

Our ship is called the Mayflower.
Over 100 people are onboard.
It is small and crowded, and sickness is all around.

PART 1 REFRAIN

THIRD COLONIST:

There is no kitchen on our ship.
Our food is cold and hard:
Biscuits, cheese, and salted meat are all we have to eat.

PART 1 REFRAIN

FOURTH COLONIST:

66 long days have passed.
Now the deck is suddenly filled!
"There's land ahead! Our voyage is complete!"

PART 2

FIFTH COLONIST:

We tied our ship to Plymouth Rock
And came upon the land.
A fierce wind blew the frost and cold.
We shivered and were hungry, too.

PART 2 REFRAIN:

The winds blew so cold,
And the food was nearly gone,
But the Pilgrims never gave up.

SIXTH COLONIST:

We chopped and we chopped until the trees fell down.
Then we sawed them all into planks.
We built our cabins one by one while the snow lay on the ground.

PART 2 REFRAIN

SEVENTH COLONIST:

Indians came, and we gave them gifts.
They showed us how to hunt.
They helped us catch some fish to eat,
For now our food was gone.

PART 2 REFRAIN

EIGHTH COLONIST:

The Indians even gave us some seed
So we could plant corn in the spring.
We plowed the Earth as soon as we could
So we'd have a good harvest that fall.

PART 2 REFRAIN

PART 3

NINTH COLONIST:
We went deep in the forest to hunt more food
And returned with turkeys and deer.
We cooked this food on our outdoor fires
And filled the air with good smells.

PART 3 REFRAIN:
Our friends have helped us,
And our crops have been gathered.
For all of these things, we give thanks.

TENTH COLONIST:
We got corn and pumpkins
And other food from the harvest ready.
There was enough for a long feast.
There was plenty, and a feast means more than enough.

PART 3 REFRAIN

ELEVENTH COLONIST:
The Indians came and stayed 3 days,
For their feasts were always this long.
We all played games while more food was prepared.
What a wonderful gathering it was!

PART 4

TWELFTH COLONIST:
Our country has grown; its people are many,
But we still choose our leaders, and
We are still free to worship as we please.

PART 4 REFRAIN:
Give thanks for the Pilgrims,
For their courage and strength.
Give thanks for the country we love.

THIRTEENTH COLONIST:
That's why we are all thankful that we can live and grow up in the
land that the Pilgrims made their home long, long ago!

PART 4 REFRAIN

Act 4

MONOLOGUES

MONOLOGUES

Introduction

A monologue is a speech performed by one person. When teaching this term, remind students that the prefix "mono" means one. Monologues are most often written from a human perspective, but they can also be written to reflect the views of animals, plants, and inanimate objects.

A well-written monologue is long enough and contains enough details for an actor to assume a personality and develop a character through actions and vocal intonation. Many acting agencies require actors to perform memorized monologues, or they may even assign a monologue for actors to prepare in a timed setting. Preparing and performing a monologue requires the actor to completely understand the character in the script and to portray that character in a believable way.

By performing monologues, students practice reading fluently, using vocal inflection, speaking at the proper rate, and speaking clearly. Monologues are written and performed to inform, entertain, express an opinion, or persuade.

Students can easily be taught to write and perform their own monologues, because monologues are narratives. Students must be able to assume the point of view of the subject and write from that perspective.

This section contains four monologues. As students perform each monologue, challenge them to answer the following questions:

- ✦ How would you describe the main character in the monologue?
- ✦ Was this monologue written to inform, entertain, express an opinion, or persuade?
- ✦ What was the main message of this monologue?

You may find other sources for monologues on the Internet. After students have performed several monologues from a variety of viewpoints, challenge them to write their own monologues. You can use this as a research opportunity for students to learn more about characters from history, or as a creative thinking activity wherein students develop a monologue from the viewpoint of an inanimate object of their choice.

WHO AM I? A MONOLOGUE WITH A TWIST

From my point of view, things look weird in your house. You think I don't pay attention, but you're wrong. When the TV is on, I watch it. When you have friends over, I watch you play. You probably don't even think about me until it's time to feed me. I wish you would think about me a little more. When's the last time you cleaned my home? I mean, I do a good job of cleaning up a bit in here, but my water is getting old, and I could use some new plants. I saw a commercial for a new castle on TV the other day. I think it would fit in my current tank. You should buy it for me. It would probably be safer than my old castle.

You know who scares me? The cat. He was looking me the other day. He likes to stand right next to my home. I think he's trying to get me. The cat just looks evil to me. I think he would eat me if he could get to me. I think if he were bigger, he would eat you, too. You should see the way he looks at you when you're not looking. I wish the cat would go outside and stay there.

I like the dog. I don't even think he knows that I'm here. I can tell that he and I are on the same page about the cat.

Write Your Own "Who Am I?" Monologue

Choose a subject or character: _____

_____

Think about three things to talk about in your monologue: _____

_____

_____

_____

Now write your monologue. Remember to write from the first-person point of view, using pronouns such as I, we, us, and me.

_____

_____

_____

_____

_____

_____

_____

_____

_____

_____

_____

_____

_____

_____

_____

_____

_____

_____

_____

_____

_____

_____

BEST DAY EVER!

I was supposed to study my spelling words last night, because I have a test today. But I didn't. I had 15 problems in math to do, but I didn't do them. I was even supposed to read my book for 30 minutes, but guess what? I didn't do that, either. Know why? I forgot my backpack at school.

I didn't even think about my homework until it was time to go to bed. When I got home yesterday, I played with my friends, watched TV—you know, the usual. Mom wasn't very happy with me when she found out. She said I wasn't responsible. But I *am* responsible. I worried about my homework all night.

So today, I got up, got dressed, and ate a bowl of cereal while watching TV. I noticed a message on the bottom of the screen. It said some schools in my area were cancelling classes that day because of ice. Sweet!

But you know my luck. The name of my school never went across the screen, so I dragged myself down the street. I was thinking it was going to be the worst day ever. I wouldn't even get recess because of the homework.

As I walked up the sidewalk, I saw my principal telling people in cars that school was cancelled. Hooray! I ran up to her and asked if I could go inside for my backpack, and she said yes! When I came outside, I skipped all the way back home, thinking, "This is the best day ever!" And, yes—I did my homework!

What was your best day ever? Write about your best day in a personal narrative format below.

_____

_____

_____

_____

_____

_____

_____

_____

_____

_____

_____

_____

_____

_____

_____

_____

_____

_____

_____

_____

_____

_____

THE SHOPPING TRIP

Mom said we have to go shopping for school clothes today. Three words in that sentence make me very unhappy. I don't like "shopping" unless it involves toys. "School" is not something I would choose to do, if I had the choice. And shopping for "clothes" is just boring.

First, Mom will drag me to a department store to try on 100 pairs of jeans to find just the right fit. Of course, they can't fit exactly right, because she says, "You need room to grow." She always tells the salesperson that I grow like a weed and she doesn't want to have to buy new jeans in October. Blah blah blah. It's the same old thing every year. So she buys me jeans that are too big in the waist and 3 inches too long. By the time I get out of school in June, the jeans fit just right. Tell me how this makes sense.

Then we go look at shirts. She always wants to buy me nice, button-down shirts. All the kids in my class wear cool T-shirts with prints and funny sayings on them. But unless I want a big fight in the store, I usually have to choose some of each. I just hang the button-down shirts in the back of my closet.

I'll be glad when we're on our way home. Mom always blabs on about what good deals we got at the stores. I'm just glad I don't have to do this for another year.

Write a personal narrative about your experiences shopping for school clothes below.

_____

_____

_____

_____

_____

_____

_____

_____

_____

_____

_____

_____

_____

_____

_____

_____

_____

_____

_____

_____

_____

FRANKLY SPEAKING

Hello. I'm Frank. I'm an owl. To be exact, I am a barn own. Yes, I know what you are thinking: Owls can't talk like humans—but let's not go there. I have some things to get off my chest.

First of all, we owls can't turn our heads all the way around like they show in cartoons. Our eyes are in the front of our heads, just like you human types. We can turn our heads pretty far, though. We can look over our left shoulders as far as about 135 degrees, and over our right shoulders about the same. So we can't see all the way around, but we can see 270 degrees. How far around can you see?

We are far-sighted, which means we can see stuff from far away. That comes in very handy for hunting. We don't see very well up close, though. When we catch our prey, we eat it whole. Whatever we can't digest, we hack up in balls called owl pellets. Yum! You may think this is gross, but we help keep the mouse and insect populations down.

Owls aren't nest builders. We like to consider ourselves recyclers. If we find an empty hole in a tree, we move in. Got an empty barn, cave, or building? We like those just fine. Any sheltered nesting site will work for us.

One last thing. What's up with calling owls wise? Not all owls are wise. Trust me. I know a few that are a couple slices short of a full loaf. I know we're used as symbols for knowledge and intelligence, but give us a break. We are just birds—beautiful birds of prey with amazing adaptations.

Write a narrative from the viewpoint of another animal below.

Act 5
STARTERS

STARTERS

Introduction

The next three Reader's Theaters are incomplete. We got you started, but students need to do some research in order to complete the scripts.

First, have students work in small groups of five or six and read the script as it is written.

Second, have students research facts that are relevant to the skit so far. The skits include independent research sheets for your convenience. Each group of students can make different additions to the skit.

Third, challenge students to find a place where they can insert their addition into the script. Make sure the filled-in script flows and sounds connected. This may require changing the line that comes right before the added material.

Encourage students to practice the play and fine-tune the script and their changes within their small groups.

Finally, have students present their finished product to the class.

A BARN WITH NO BOUNDARIES

Note to Teacher

✦ There are 14 parts in this play. Assign parts, then let students practice reading, first silently and then to a partner. Avoid asking students to read aloud without time to practice.

✦ At the conclusion of the Reader's Theater, challenge students to add more characters, rewrite some of the parts, or to analyze the humor (why was it funny?).

Cast of Characters

Farmer

Cat

Pig

Dog

Kitten

Sheep

Chicken

Rooster

Horse

Donkey

Goat

Snake

Cow

Owl

Setting

A barn full of animals who have just arrived and been crammed into the same space, without separate accommodations

Optional Props

Signs worn by actors to identify their characters

Farmer: Welcome to your new home. I know you'll all enjoy living here. I haven't had time to make you pens yet, but I'm sure you'll get along. (*petting the dog*) See you later!

Cat: Who's he kidding? I can't live next to THAT! (*points at pig*)

Pig: Can't help the mud and the snorting—those come with the territory of being a pig.

Dog: Well, you don't have to go tracking all that mud through the barn!

Kitten: Mommy! Mommy! Look at my fur! It's all muddy, and mud tastes horrible! (*spitting*)

Pig: Speaking of fur, look at all those hairballs you and your kitten have coughed up. They're everywhere! Keep your coughing to yourselves!

Sheep: This is a baa-aa-aa-d place to live. It already stinks, because we have no designated restroom areas.

Dog: Hey, man, I'm just marking my territory.

Chicken: Well, my nest is NOT your territory, sir!

Rooster: Yes, you and your "territory" need to take it outside.

Horse: I don't like sharing this barn with any of you. The cat prowls and the dog howls all night. How am I supposed to get any sleep?

Donkey: You think you've got it bad? With these ears, I hear everything, including the goat, munching that can ALL NIGHT LONG!

Goat: (*nervously*) I can't help it. I hate snakes, and that one slithers all over this barn at night.

Chicken: Not in my nest or near my eggs—EVER!

Snake: Sssay, sssister, I get my mealsss elsssewhere. And besssides, I lived in thisss barn way before any of you came along.

Cow: Well, it's obvious that what we need around here are some rules. And since I'm the smartest animal here—(*interrupted by animals*)

Animals: Hey, you're not smartest! Who left you in charge? This is not a dictatorship! (*grunting, growling, crowing, other angry animal noises*)

Owl: Whooo! Whooo! You people sure do make a lot of noise so early in the morning! What's the matter with you? Can't you see I'm trying to sleep?

Horse: Who sleeps in the daytime? It's the perfect time for grazing.

Owl: I'm nocturnal, and I don't plan to listen to all this bickering every morning as I'm trying to sleep. The cow is right. You do need some rules if you're going to live together in this barn without driving yourselves crazy.

Dog: Yeah? Well, who's gonna be in charge of making these rules? I'm not listening to a CAT!

Cat: I won't take orders from a pig!

Horse: I'm far superior to a donkey!

Owl: That's enough. You need to work together to elect a leader and create rules for the barn.

To Be Continued . . .

DEFEND YOURSELF!

Note to Teacher

✦ This Reader's Theater is incomplete. Students will need to research animals and write their own lines before performing this play.

Cast of Characters

Roly-Poly Pill Bug (narrator)
Rattlesnake
Other animals
Lion

Setting

Animal Defense Convention

Roly-Poly Pill Bug: I'm so excited! I'm finally here—the first Animal Defense Convention. This is my big chance. I can find out about all of the ways other animals protect themselves against predators, especially humans.

Rattlesnake: Hi, Roly! (*laughs*)

Roly-Poly Pill Bug: Hi, Rattlesnake! What are you doing here? (*sounding envious*) You already have great protection.

Rattlesnake: I know—the greatest set of defenses, in my opinion. I can hear people coming by listening to the vibrations my jawbone sends to my inner ear. I can strike quickly or hang back and make scary noises. I have great camouflage, and don't forget my fearsome fangs and venom.

Roly-Poly Pill Bug: Then why are you here?

Rattlesnake: I guess you could call me a role model. I also like to show off and help other animals pick out or change their survival equipment and defense "tricks."

Roly-Poly Pill Bug: Well, can you help me? How would I look with fangs? What about a rattle?

Rattlesnake: No, I don't think fangs and rattles are for you. I have to go now—the convention is beginning. Why don't you ask some other animals at the convention how they survive? Maybe some other kind of protection will suit you.

Roly-Poly Pill Bug: (*comes up to a group of animals, clears throat*) Excuse me! May I ask how you defend yourselves?

Animal 1:

Animal 2:

Animal 3:

Animal 4:

Animal 5:

Animal 6:

Animal 7:

Roly-Poly Pill Bug: These sound very interesting, but so far, I don't think any of these kinds of defenses are for me. I'd better ask some other animals what they do. (*rolling up to another group of animals*) Excuse me, but what solutions do you have for self-defense?

Animal 8:

Animal 9:

Animal 10:

Animal 11:

(more or fewer animals as needed for everyone to have a part)

At the same convention, 2 days later . . .

Lion: (*to Roly-Poly Pill Bug*) Well, little buddy, the convention is almost over. Have you made a decision yet?

Roly-Poly Pill Bug: Yes, I've decided to go with poison that I spit from my legs. Then I'm going to add spikes all over my body so that I can inflict pain when anybody tries to touch me. Furthermore, I'm going to let out an incredible screeching sound that pierces through the air and stuns anyone within 2 miles if they come anywhere near me. What do you think?

Lion: (*sarcastically, but with a grin*) Is that ALL?

Roly-Poly Pill Bug: Yeah! I think that will about do it. I guess I'll go put in my order now.

BOOMING ANNOUNCEMENT: The convention is now officially over. Thank you for coming. Have a SAFE trip home.

(*DOOR SLAMS SHUT*)

Roly-Poly Pill Bug: (*sobbing*) No! No! No! You can't mean it! Not over! Please let me in! It's a matter of life and death! I'll only be a minute!

Lion: Don't worry, little buddy, there's always next year. In the meantime, just roll up in a really tight ball whenever you get scared. (*snickers and walks away*)

Roly-Poly Pill Bug: Well, you can laugh now, but wait until next year. Just wait until you see me then. I'll be big and bad! (*rolls off*)

ANIMAL DEFENSES INDEPENDENT RESEARCH

Select an animal and research what the animal uses for defense against predators. Use the following research form.

Animal: _____

Animal's method(s) of defending itself against predators and dangers: _____

_____

_____

How defense works: _____

_____

_____

Script to be inserted in the Reader's Theater:_____

_____

_____

_____

_____

_____

_____

Where should the script be inserted, and how does it connect to the flow of the play? _____

_____

_____

SUPER NUT MAN!

Cast of Characters
Teacher
Super Nut Man
Veggie Breath
Additional characters as inserted

Setting
Classroom

Optional Props
Color transparency or poster of
food pyramid (newest version)

Teacher: Today we are fortunate enough to have Super Nut Man and his side kick Veggie Breath with us to introduce our next unit of study.

Super Nut Man: (*acting insulted*) Excuse me . . . it is pronounced Super NEWT Man, as in NU-tri-tion. Not NUT, like a peanut.

Teacher: Oh, excuse me. Can I just call you "Newt," then?

Super Nut Man: No, you can call me "Super."

Teacher: OK . . . Super . . . Would you like to start by explaining to the class why you and Veggie Breath are here?

Super Nut Man: Yes, I will. Breath and I are alarmed at what we read in the papers and see on the news these days about the poor eating habits of Americans—adults and children both.

Veggie Breath: We're alarmed not only by WHAT they eat, but also by how much they eat, and by how inactive they are!

Super Nut Man: But don't worry. I am here to explain the food pyramid, and I'm sure I'll make it as clear as mud.

Teacher: Don't you mean crystal clear?

Super Nut Man: (*startled*) Yes, of course that's what I mean. Please don't interrupt—I might get startled and accidentally run away. I have lightning reflexes, you know.

Veggie Breath: (*speaking very close to Super Nut Man*) Did you get your lightning reflexes from following the food pyramid?

Super Nut Man: Why, yes. (*covers nose*) Please never talk to me that close again. I sure wish your brother, Fruit Breath, hadn't retired.

Teacher: Can we get back to the food pyramid?

Super Nut Man: I would, but I must eat a piece of low fat cheese immediately, because my blood sugar is low. You take over, Breath.

Veggie Breath: OK! As you can see, there are six columns, all different colors. (*show color transparency or poster of newest food pyramid*) These colors represent the five different food groups, plus oil.

Super Nut Man: I'm not drinking motor oil! That's disgusting! Is that why your breath is so bad?

Veggie Breath: Not motor oil, food oil. Like oil found in olives, fish, and nuts. And for your information, my breath is bad because I need two AA batteries for my toothbrush, and all I have is one battery.

Super Nut Man: (*confused*) Why are some stripes in the food pyramid wider than others? (*pauses and tries to act confident*) Obviously, I already know—I'm just testing you.

Veggie Breath: The different sizes help remind you to choose more foods from certain groups and less from others. You should try to follow this guide every day.

NOTE: Here, students should insert their scripts about various healthy foods. They can write scripts using Veggie Breath, Super Nut, and the Teacher, or they can add additional characters, such as foods speaking for themselves or students responding to the characters in the play.

Veggie Breath: You should also do something active every day, too.

Super Nut Man: Active? I've got you there. I skateboard with Tony Hawk every day.

Veggie Breath: You know Tony Hawk?

Super Nut Man: Yes, he lives in my living room—in a little box that's plugged into the TV. I have no idea how he fits in there!

Veggie Breath: Playing a video game does not count as being active. Go running, take walks, play outside, swim, bike, or walk up the stairs instead of using elevators.

Super Nut Man: I might just do all of those things today—except I won't take the stairs. I really love elevators.

Veggie Breath: You don't need to change overnight. Just start by doing one good thing you don't usually do, and go from there.

Super Nut Man: (*to class*) That wraps it up! I hope I was able to make the food pyramid clear.

Teacher: Well, class, let's give Veggie Breath and his sidekick Super Nut a big round of applause.

Super Nut Man: No, Veggie Breath is MY sidekick. You're funny!

Teacher: I was not trying to be funny.

Super Nut Man: My work here is done, Veggie Breath. Let's ride—or walk, or run, or skip. Or maybe you can carry me!

Veggie Breath: I'm not carrying you again.

(*both exit*)

Reader's Theater for Grades 3–4 © Taylor & Francis Groups. • Permission is granted to photocopy or reproduce this page for single classroom use only.

HEALTH AND NUTRITION INDEPENDENT RESEARCH

Select a healthy food to research. What are the health benefits of eating this food? What is the correct portion size, and how should it be cooked or served? Use the following research form.

Food: _____

Health benefit(s): _____

_____

Portion size of this food: _____

_____

Way this food should be cooked or served: _____

_____

Script to be inserted in Reader's Theater: _____

_____

_____

_____

_____

_____

Where should the script be inserted, and how does it connect to the flow of

the play? _____

_____

_____

READER'S THEATER RUBRIC

Student or Team: _____

Topic or Title: _____

Directions: Mark the appropriate rating for each criterion. Use these individual ratings to assign an overall rating for the assignment.

Criteria	0 Working on It!	1 Novice	2 Acceptable	3 Out of the Box!
Uses Prewriting Strategies	Cannot generate prewriting graphic organizers, notes, or brainstorming	Some use of prewriting in the form of organizers, notes, or brainstorming	Use of more than one prewriting strategy; mostly well-organized and thought-out	Numerous strategies used and followed to create a well-organized and thought-out composition
Content Is Valid and Accurate	Content is shallow and shows no insight	Content is accurate but lacks insight; few supporting examples	Content is accurate with some questions left unanswered and a few supporting examples	Content is 100% accurate and has supporting examples
Creativity	Could not express or present information	Presentation lacked creativity	Presentation moderately creative, entertaining, and informative	Engaging presentation that was creative, entertaining, and informative

Comments: _____

_____

_____

BLANK RUBRIC

Student or Team: _____

Topic or Title: _____

Directions: Mark the appropriate rating for each criterion. Use these individual ratings to assign an overall rating for the assignment.

Criteria	0 Working on it!	1 Novice	2 Acceptable	3 Out of the Box!	Not Applicable

Comments: _____

_____

_____

ABOUT THE AUTHORS

Brenda McGee was an award-winning classroom teacher for 18 years in North Carolina and Texas. Her degrees include a B.S. from Elon University, an M.Ed. from the University of North Carolina at Greensboro, and post-master's work in curriculum development at the University of North Texas at Denton. Brenda started publishing in 1975 and is the author of hundreds of teaching ideas, materials, manipulatives, and books used in regular, special education, and gifted classrooms. She cofounded McGee-Keiser Academic Enrichment Programs, acquired by Prufrock Press in 2007. After a brief, one-year retirement, Brenda is back developing curriculum for an international company, Time to Know, Inc., and she is working on several other independent projects. Known for her sense of humor, Brenda has been a guest speaker, consultant, and presenter at numerous conferences and workshops across the country.

Debbie Keiser is an award-winning curriculum writer who taught for several years as a gifted and talented cluster teacher and facilitator. She earned her undergraduate degree from Texas Tech University and her M.Ed. in educational psychology, with an emphasis in gifted education, from the University of North Texas at Denton. She has been publishing since 1996 and has numerous titles to her credit for both regular and gifted education. She is also passionate about dyslexia research and has led many afterschool sessions for parents, teachers, and students on this subject. She cofounded McGee-Keiser Academic Enrichment Programs, acquired by Prufrock Press in 2007. Debbie is currently developing curriculum for an international company, Time to Know, Inc. and is writing a book to help parents whose children are affected by dyslexia. Debbie has been a keynote speaker and has presented numerous conference sessions and workshops at the local, state, national, and international levels.

COMMON CORE STATE STANDARDS ALIGNMENT

Grade Level	Common Core State Standards
Grade 3 ELA-Literacy	RL.3.3 Describe characters in a story (e.g., their traits, motivations, or feelings) and explain how their actions contribute to the sequence of events.
	RL.3.4 Determine the meaning of words and phrases as they are used in a text, distinguishing literal from nonliteral language.
	RF.3.3 Know and apply grade-level phonics and word analysis skills in decoding words.
	RF.3.4 Read with sufficient accuracy and fluency to support comprehension.
	SL.3.2 Determine the main ideas and supporting details of a text read aloud or information presented in diverse media and formats, including visually, quantitatively, and orally.
	SL.3.4 Report on a topic or text, tell a story, or recount an experience with appropriate facts and relevant, descriptive details, speaking clearly at an understandable pace.
	L.3.4 Determine or clarify the meaning of unknown and multiple-meaning word and phrases based on grade 3 reading and content, choosing flexibly from a range of strategies.
Grade 4 ELA-Literacy	RL.4.1 Refer to details and examples in a text when explaining what the text says explicitly and when drawing inferences from the text.
	RL.4.2 Determine a theme of a story, drama, or poem from details in the text; summarize the text.
	RL.4.3 Describe in depth a character, setting, or event in a story or drama, drawing on specific details in the text (e.g., a character's thoughts, words, or actions).
	RL.4.4 Determine the meaning of words and phrases as they are used in a text, including those that allude to significant characters found in mythology (e.g., Herculean).
	RF.3.3 Know and apply grade-level phonics and word analysis skills in decoding words.
	RF.3.4 Read with sufficient accuracy and fluency to support comprehension.
	SL.4.2 Paraphrase portions of a text read aloud or information presented in diverse media and formats, including visually, quantitatively, and orally.
	SL.4.4 Report on a topic or text, tell a story, or recount an experience in an organized manner, using appropriate facts and relevant, descriptive details to support main ideas or themes; speak clearly at an understandable pace.
	L.4.4 Determine or clarify the meaning of unknown and multiple-meaning words and phrases based on grade 4 reading and content, choosing flexibly from a range of strategies.
Grade 5 ELA-Literacy	RL.5.1 Quote accurately from a text when explaining what the text says explicitly and when drawing inferences from the text.
	RL.5.2 Determine a theme of a story, drama, or poem from details in the text, including how characters in a story or drama respond to challenges or how the speaker in a poem reflects upon a topic; summarize the text.
	RL.5.3 Compare and contrast two or more characters, settings, or events in a story or drama, drawing on specific details in the text (e.g., how characters interact).
	RL.5.4 Determine the meaning of words and phrases as they are used in a text, including figurative language such as metaphors and similes.
	SL.5.2 Summarize a written text read aloud or information presented in diverse media and formats, including visually, quantitatively, and orally.

Printed in the United States
by Baker & Taylor Publisher Services